JOURNEY

TO

Acceptance

TWO JOURNEYS, ONE TAPESTRY
OF GENDER RECOGNITION

TRACY TURNER

To my two wonderful daughters.
And to my genuine friends, both old and new – you know
who you are.

CONTENTS

PART ONE: EL'S JOURNEY

PART TWO: MY JOURNEY

PART THREE: OUR JOURNEY

APPENDIXES

PREFACE

This is a mother's memoir of her daughter's transgender journey.

I am not a professional expert on what it means to be transgender, and I do not pretend to know all the issues that young trans adults may encounter. This is just an honest account of my journey with my daughter: an honest recollection of my thoughts and reactions, and the consequences that ultimately guided me to a different place in my life.

I have included some legal information where I felt it served a purpose, but I have steered away from trying to defend or prove one opinion over another. Defending personal opinions is not why I wrote this book. My aspiration was to write the kind of book that would have aided me on my own journey if I'd had it.

It's not my intention to sway people's opinions on transgender issues. I believe in everyone's right to choose, as long as their choice does not harm another. I believe in equal rights for all, in women's rights, and in promoting the safety of our children. It's my hope that when you read this story, it will open your heart to the belief that we can all live together whatever our differences, and that compassion, understanding, and empathy should be the way forward for all of us.

I've changed names throughout this book to protect family and friends from those who may wish to harm members of this marginalised community or their supporters. I pray that one day soon this necessity will no longer exist, but for now, it does.

At the end of the book, I have listed some resources that provide help and information that I found useful. Most inspired me; all were integral to my journey. Please look at these for further information should you wish.

A note on pronoun usage throughout the narrative: I will address my child as 'my son' or 'Billy' before his transition and when he briefly detransitions. Otherwise, I will use her chosen name, El. When El is telling me of her past feelings and experiences, I will refer to her as 'she', as she is now, although she will talk about times when she was Billy.

Information gleaned from books and speech and information recently shared with me by El is presented in italics.

GRATITUDE

I want to share this story about my daughter's journey, a journey that has enlightened and enriched my world, allowing me to forge a bond with my two daughters that might not have existed without the path we travelled together.

I want to let other parents know that it's okay to think and even say the things that appear in your head. It's permissible to feel your emotions, doubt yourself, and even be selfish and judgemental at times. You are human, vulnerable, and defined by your beliefs and society.

Allow yourself to be angry, hurt, and truthful, but also be compassionate, kind, and open to change. Life has a way of transforming your pain and suffering into gratitude, understanding, and strength. It can open doors you never imagined, leading you to a peaceful existence you'll cherish.

I hope this honest account of my feelings and actions as a parent of a transgender individual will help other parents on their journey.

And I hope you enjoy it.

Throughout this journey, I found inspiration in the words of Theodore Roosevelt:

It is not the critic who counts; not the man who points out how the strong man stumbles, or where the doer of deeds could have done them better. The credit belongs to the man who is actually in the arena, whose face is marred by dust and sweat and blood; who strives valiantly; who errs, who comes short again and again, because there is no effort without error and shortcoming; but who does actually strive to do the deeds; who knows great enthusiasms, the great devotions; who spends himself in a worthy cause; who at the best knows in the end the triumph of high achievement, and who at the worst, if he fails, at least fails while daring greatly.

I discovered this quote while reading Brené Brown's book *Daring Greatly*, and it captures the essence of her book. The book is a must-read, and the message resonated with me so deeply that I adopted 'dare greatly' as my personal mantra.

Credit belongs to El, who dared to be in the arena, who fought for her authenticity. Those nameless individuals who criticise do not count.

GENDER IDENTITY

What is gender identity?

According to the National Society for the Prevention of Cruelty to Children, gender identity describes a person's internal sense of being male, female, or something else entirely. For many people, this internal sense aligns with the sex they were assigned at birth. However, for others, it does not. Some people experience gender identity as existing on a spectrum, rather than as strictly being male or female.

There are many other expressions of gender identity. Some individuals identify as non-binary or gender-fluid. For others, the concept of gender isn't relevant to their identity. Gender identity is a personal feeling, and a child or young person will be best positioned to know which identifier matches how they feel. Children and young people can also question or feel unsure about their gender identity, or they may find that their gender identity changes.

Gender Dysphoria

The National Society for the Prevention of Cruelty to Children defines gender dysphoria as when someone experiences unease because their gender identity differs from, or doesn't sit comfortably with, the sex they were assigned at birth. Gender dysphoria is not a mental illness, but some people may develop mental health problems, such as depression or anxiety, because of gender dysphoria.

Types of Gender Identity

A young person or child might use various terms to describe their gender identity. These include the following:

- **Trans or transgender:** These terms are used when someone feels their gender differs from, or doesn't sit comfortably with, the sex they were assigned at birth.
- **Non-binary, gender diverse, and genderqueer:** These are umbrella terms for people whose gender identity doesn't fit comfortably as male or female. Instead, they may identify with some aspects of one or both identities, or identify with neither. Some people may identify as gender-fluid and see their gender as flexible, rather than as a fixed identity.
- **Cisgender:** This term is used to refer to someone when their gender identity is the same as the sex they were assigned at birth.

EL'S REVELATION

January 2014 is indelibly marked in my memory, a time that will never be forgotten. When my son Billy, then seventeen, approached me with a request to sit down, my breath caught in my throat. A tremor of nervous anticipation ran through me, a nervous energy that buzzed beneath my skin. My heart was racing, and my palms were sweaty. I reminded myself to breathe. I did not know what Billy was going to tell me. As my mind raced, I considered various scenarios, from having a pregnant girlfriend to the revelation that he might be gay. Surprisingly, the idea of his being transgender never entered my thoughts, although I had contemplated the possibility of his being gay. Had I ignored some signs? Had I kept my observations to myself? Thinking back now, I wonder.

With quiet determination, my child – who was not Billy, I soon learned, but a woman named El – shared her lived experience, her eyes reflecting the depth of her understanding of her identity as a girl, a conviction that had shaped her from a young age, a truth she held close to her heart. El spoke about her attempts to navigate these feelings by hiding them, suppressing them, and wishing them away. She described a lifelong discomfort with her body, a feeling of being out of place, like a square peg in a round hole, and a sense of never truly belonging.

While discussing her sex, her body, and expected social roles to me, El cried. Her immense pain was hard to witness. Her difficulties in social situations, previously hinted at, crystallised with this shared understanding, revealing a pattern of misunderstandings on my part. El had known for a long time that she wasn't like other boys. She didn't wish to be; she yearned to be seen and recognised as a woman. It was so unexpected that I was left dumbfounded, a stunned silence replacing any coherent thought or words. The pain in my heart was a physical weight, my muscles tensed involuntarily, and nausea gripped my stomach. The shock of El's revelation, a seismic shift in my understanding of everything, would resonate with me for the next decade.

PART ONE:

EL'S JOURNEY

1

THE EARLY YEARS

My son Billy, born in Truro, Cornwall, in July 1996, earned the affectionate nickname 'Cornish Pasty' early on. Even as a newborn, Billy displayed an impressive stubborn streak. Hours of meticulous preparation at home, following my well-researched birth plan, went out the window with his arrival. My son, it seemed, had his own schedule: it was a two-hour whirlwind from my first contraction to his first cry. The hospital room blurred into view, my carefully crafted pain management techniques abandoned in the passenger seat. Nevertheless, my ultimate focus lay on the healthy baby boy cradled in my arms.

Billy was a dynamo of a baby, thriving on constant attention. He demanded to be held, rocked, or fed what seemed like every hour. Sleep became a distant memory, replaced by a blur of nappy changes and lullabies. Nights presented challenges, as a constant cycle of rocking and feeding persisted until the first light of dawn appeared through the curtains. He'd fight sleep with everything he had, little fists clenched and eyes bloodshot with fatigue, determined to stay awake. Yet the situation evoked not only frustration but a peculiar charm.

The night Billy finally slept through, I swear I didn't sleep at all. Exhaustion warred with disbelief as the clock ticked past his usual wake-up time. Eventually I entered his room and examined his tiny chest to verify he was breathing.

This little human possessed unwavering determination, a quality that would serve him well in the years to come.

Josie, my firstborn, exemplified a true contrast. An angel in baby form, she slept through the night from day one. She cried infrequently and was easily calmed, and her sunny disposition always brought a smile to my face. However, Billy showcased a remarkable force of nature. He craved constant attention, his cries could pierce the strongest eardrums, and sleep seemed like a foreign concept to him.

While taking care of Josie came naturally, Billy demanded a novel approach. Lesson learned: every child is an individual, and what worked for one won't work for another. Despite their differences, I loved both these minor miracles.

Mealtime Mayhem

Mealtimes with Billy were an exercise in frustration. He'd guzzle down bottles of milk; however, pureed food was the enemy. We tried every trick in the book – colourful plates, silly faces, airplane noises – but nothing worked. Going out to eat with him was demanding, ultimately making even a casual brunch into a challenging negotiation.

One trying evening, my resourceful sister announced bath time with a mischievous glint in her eye. The bathtub became a makeshift highchair, Billy surrounded by his favourite bath toys. As he was engrossed in splashing and playing, my sister, with the precision of a surgeon, would shovel spoonsful of pureed peas into his mouth. To my astonishment, it worked. The distraction of the toys combined with the novelty of the situation had Billy gobbling down his entire meal.

Sunshine and Setbacks

Family vacations with my sister and friends had always stood out as a highlight of the year. Sun-drenched beaches, laughter-filled evenings, and the joy of watching the kids splash in the sea – those were my memories of our time together. One year, however, stood out from the rest. Billy's apprehension about the water kept him firmly planted on the sand. While the others revelled in the cool waves, I played in a tiny paddling pool with Billy.

Billy's fear of the sea posed an unforeseen obstacle. I confess, I found it frustrating at first. But Billy, a picture of defiance in his brightly coloured swim floats, remained rooted to the sand, his chin jutting out in a display of stubbornness that rivalled a mule's.

Acceptance came on the dawn of the holiday's last day. I had resigned myself to a beach getaway with no sea fun for Billy. To my astonishment, he toddled over to the water's edge with mischief in his eye and exclaimed, 'Water!' Soon after, he transformed into a bundle of laughter and wild movements, happily splashing around in the water alongside his cousins and sister.

Even at the tender age of two, Billy possessed a spirit as independent as the ocean itself. His will of iron didn't always prove easy to navigate, but it unquestionably contributed to his charm. This beach trip exemplified a single instance of his unwavering determination. The little boy who challenged the sea on that last day provided a glimpse of the strong, independent person he would develop into.

School Days: A Baptism by Fire

Billy, just three years old, began his education at the local Truro primary school, a place filled with the colourful artwork of his classmates and the exciting chatter of his peers. However, Billy's initiation into school turned out to be difficult. The structured environment, with its emphasis on group activities and singalongs, clashed spectacularly with his independent spirit.

To put it mildly, Billy's behaviour lacked predictability during his school days. His unwavering determination to forge his own path often manifested in the most inconvenient ways, like refusing to budge from under a classroom table. The phone's ring frequently broke the peacefulness of my workday, the principal's voice revealing a mix of amusement and concern.

With a sigh and a silent apology to my overflowing inbox, I'd race to school, hoping to entice Billy from his refuge. The sight of a pair of tiny legs sticking out from under a colourful table became a familiar, albeit slightly comical, scene at Billy's school.

The teachers, bless their patient hearts, took it all in stride. One day, it might be Ms Jackson trying to coax him out with a funny voice; another day, Mr Davies would attempt to lure him with the promise of building a giant block tower together. Personally, I used a combination of bribery (with a new toy) and a promise of an exciting playground adventure after school.

Despite his stubborn streak and penchant for under-the-table protests, Billy's heart overflowed with kindness. He'd share his toys with other children, his tiny face etched with concern if a classmate experienced sadness. Even at that age, his gentle nature drew animals to him, revealing his deep love for them. Billy's personality embodied a beautiful paradox – a tornado of independence enveloping a core of pure gentleness. I loved my little guy!

Nature, Nurture, and Fairy Wings

Pondering Billy's childhood today, I'm left with a lingering question. Did these glimpses of his independent spirit show early signs of his gender identity, or do they just reflect a unique and determined personality? The truth, I believe, lies somewhere in between: my child is a beautiful tapestry woven from nature and nurture, defiance and self-discovery.

One memory of Billy, etched vividly in my mind, involves a pair of sparkly pink fairy wings. When my children were both young, someone gifted Josie, Billy's sister, with these wings for Christmas. However, Billy, with unwavering determination, claimed them as his own. He spent countless hours flitting around the house, adorned with these wings. Any attempt to remove them, even at bathtime or bedtime, proved to be a formidable struggle.

'It's all right for him to play with pink fairy wings,' I would assure his father, gently reminding him that Josie, during her younger years, preferred short hair and clothing typically associated with boys. I believed, and still do, that fostering self-expression is an essential aspect of nurturing a child.

Strong Will, Evolving Memories

When he was four, Billy's social circle was mainly composed of boys. He also had a new fixation with his Spider-Man outfit. Like the fairy wings, he wouldn't part with it, forcing me to wait until he slept to wash it. His willpower often required me to get creative and find unconventional ways to motivate him and encourage cooperation. Despite sometimes being difficult, he showed remarkable determination at his young age.

When Billy revealed his identity to me at seventeen, his childhood memories would take on an unsettling light for me. Had I missed subtle signs? Perhaps in the cyclone of those early years, clues slipped by unnoticed. Back then, a nanny looked after Billy and Josie while I ran my business. Now I wonder whether if I were more relaxed and less focused on financial improvement, I would have picked up on these. The possibility weighs on me.

As Billy matured, he displayed occasional outbursts of anger. He was sensitive and occasionally shy, especially in crowded environments. While I noticed these traits, I attributed them to normal development and didn't perceive them as a cause for concern. Of course, these could have served as possible indicators of gender dysphoria, but neither my partner nor I had any inkling that anything like that existed.

Shifting Social Circle

During the summer, our home buzzed with activity as my nieces and nephews visited. We spent delightful days building sandcastles and splashing in the waves, or exploring the sun-drenched fields surrounding the house. Billy enjoyed a close bond with his older cousins, who often looked after him. However, as they matured, Billy's social circle noticeably shrunk. Notably, he struggled in family environments, often opting out of gatherings.

People commented on Billy, often trying to be kind, but their observations ('not very outgoing', 'unsociable', 'a loner') stung, despite the intended kindness. Unlike some accounts I'd read about young transgender individuals, Billy's historic journey offered no clear signs or warning shots to prepare me for his later revelation. For us, we perceived life unfolding as it should, with a feeling of normalcy.

Billy's sister, Josie, mirrored my own experiences as a young child by embracing a 'tomboy' phase, preferring short hair and boys' clothes. This resonated with my youth; my mother had grappled with my preference for masculine attire and activities during my upbringing. Perhaps this instilled in me an open mind regarding personal expression. However, Billy exhibited no early signs of wanting to wear girls' clothing or identify as female.

However, we seem to have lost the concept of the 'tomboy', and in its place are an endless litany of sexual and gender identities. Although I excelled at sports and preferred the company of boys, I never felt uncomfortable with my body. Although I found friendships with girls unnerving and they triggered alarms of sudden offence, I never wanted to be a boy.

As a parent, I didn't enforce stereotypical expectations for my children. They had the freedom to express themselves, and I considered their preferences when making choices about their clothing. Josie showcased a flair for fashion even at a young age, consistently gravitated towards the boys' section, and looked great in her chosen outfits.

2

UPROOTED AND UNSETTLED

When Billy was six, his father and I separated. This tough decision meant Billy, his sister Josie, and I would leave our familiar surroundings and move to the Midlands to be closer to family. While this move aimed to provide a support system during a challenging emotional period, it proved distressing for everyone, particularly Billy.

We settled into temporary housing while I navigated the complexities of securing finances for a permanent home and enrolling both children in new schools. This resulted in several unsettling moves within a short time frame, further compounding the stress and disruption for Billy.

Struggling with the upheaval, Billy displayed anger and aggression at his new school. He grappled with isolation, often withdrawing from classroom activities and exhibiting, not surprisingly, stubbornness. His withdrawal led to frequent meetings with school officials, while I advocated for him and his needs.

As months passed at his new school, Billy's social circle remained limited. His unhappiness was clear, leaving me at a loss for solutions. Unfortunately, the school offered limited practical help, and I vehemently opposed any attempts to label him based solely on his emotional struggles. Billy's intellectual capabilities were never in question; he was a bright child.

I knew and loved my son for his gentle, kind, and compassionate nature. While his sadness was apparent, I attributed it to the family separation and the unsettling year we had all endured. However, his tendency to spend hours alone in his room playing video games concerned me. He didn't engage in outdoor play or seek connection with other children, seemingly preferring solitude. Unfortunately, any attempts to encourage socialisation met with limited enthusiasm, and my concern about his potential isolation grew.

Soon, I resorted to strategies such as enrolling him in activities: Scouts, judo, karate, and other sports, each requiring dedicated uniforms and equipment. Optimistically, I hoped one might spark an interest, but none held his attention beyond a couple of weeks.

While he enjoyed playing football, he never took part in any local teams outside of school. His interests revolved around solitary activities or online gaming with friends. This self-imposed isolation, coupled with his difficulties at school, fuelled my growing worry.

In a recent conversation with El, she revealed that at six, she wasn't consciously aware of wanting to be a woman. Instead, a general sense of unhappiness and not fitting in permeated her experience. Although she had friends, she felt she was acting and conforming to expectations. This facade crumbled when she reflected on it, leaving her feeling confused and scared.

El's recent revelations about her childhood experiences resonated deeply with me. While the memories of her early years may not have explicitly pointed towards her identity as a transgender woman, the underlying emotional current – the sense of unease, the struggle to fit in – was clear. It seemed that the defiance I perceived as stubbornness may have been an attempt to break free from a mould that never felt right.

El further shared that she reached clarity only much later in life. She acknowledges she expressed some of her anger and sadness about her father's absence from the household during that time.

A Cry for Help

As Billy's struggles continued, his anger and aggression escalated, particularly at school. Incidents such as biting a teacher, pushing classmates, and even throwing a chair became disturbingly commonplace. Unfortunately, these outbursts extended to his home life, and after one upsetting episode when he kicked me in frustration, my desperation caused me to seek help from our general practitioner (GP). Soon, Billy was referred for counselling.

During one session, Billy's therapist prompted him to draw his safe place. Naturally, I expected a picture of his bedroom or a familiar space at home. However, a surge of concern washed over me as I saw his drawing – an island surrounded by a vast expanse of water. This sparked a conversation during which I tried to delve deeper into his feelings and understand what made him feel secure. But on this occasion, I couldn't quite grasp the source of his sadness.

Afterwards, Billy's drawing, a stark island with a single cabin and solitary gate, hung crookedly on the refrigerator. The endless blue ocean surrounding it only emphasised his isolation. Most notable was the depiction of a single gate and surrounding fence, drawn with a bold, dark crayon, seemingly expressing his desire for barriers. This simple yet evocative image overwhelmed me with a profound sense of sadness. What did this safe space represent for Billy? Was it a refuge from an overwhelming world or a lonely fortress built for one? I did not know what was causing my son so much pain, and I struggled to find ways that might provide me with the answers.

El revealed that the isolated island represented a yearning for a safe haven. Confused and grappling with her inner world, she felt alone and isolated, lashing out in frustration. The drawing symbolised a place where she could exert control, choosing who entered and exited her world. It was a refuge where she could feel secure, a space where the confusion and loneliness wouldn't feel so overwhelming. Ultimately, she just wanted to be alone; in a group, she felt inadequate, small, and minimised.

Ten years later, El's explanation of Billy's drawing would hang heavy in the air. Had I created a safe space, perhaps her sadness and isolation wouldn't have manifested as anger and lashing out. For me, the isolated island, once a cause of quiet sadness, would transform into a symbol of her inner turmoil. My guilt over not recognising her struggles threatened to drown me in a tidal wave of what-ifs and could-have-beens. Most important, how could I have missed this?

During other therapy sessions, Billy bravely attempted to express his internal conflict. He articulated that he felt as though there were two distinct selves within him: 'Angry Billy' and 'Billy'.

Angry Billy

Because of this, the therapists at Billy's sessions introduced a clever technique to help him navigate his emotional turmoil. They encouraged him to draw a picture of Angry Billy – a visual representation of the frustration and rage that sometimes bubbled up inside him. This drawing, proudly displayed on his bedroom door, became a communication tool. When anger threatened to overwhelm him, he could simply point to the picture, a silent yet effective way of saying 'I'm feeling angry right now.'

Often, Billy seemed like a house divided, a constant battle raging within. The 'normal Billy' – playful, kind, and eager to please his mum – existed alongside Angry Billy, a whirlwind of frustration lashing out in unpredictable outbursts. The transition between these states was like a switch flipping, with a surge of emotions overwhelming him. One moment he'd be laughing with his friends; the next, a minor trigger or a mounting sense of frustration would spark a fiery transformation into Angry Billy.

The waves of regret that washed over Billy after his outbursts were a constant reminder of the destructive nature of Angry Billy. Living with this constant internal battle wasn't easy for either of us. For Billy, the need to be 'good' and not cause me stress often led to outbursts, which were a pressure valve releasing anger. For me, it was like walking on eggshells, worrying that a moment of lapsed judgement on my part would cause Angry Billy to rear his unwelcome head once again.

Billy, at just seven years old, expressed confusion and fear about this part of himself, which

Billy aged 7

he couldn't grasp or understand. Although I tried, I was at a loss for the cause of his pain and ultimately his behaviour. His frequent desire to isolate in his room, seeking solitude or perhaps hiding from the turmoil within him, was difficult for me to fathom or understand. I was often impatient and irritated with him regarding his self-imposed isolation. I tried to understand Billy's need to be alone, but it worried and confused me. It was a phase I hoped he would eventually grow out of.

While Billy seemed calmer after his counselling sessions, addressing his ongoing challenges at school remained a significant concern.

SEEKING SOLUTIONS

Because of Billy's persistent unhappiness at school, I explored the possibility of a smaller, private school despite the significant challenge it would present as a single mother managing finances and logistics for two separate schools. Billy's father and I, believing that an environment similar to that of his Truro school could ease his transition, reached a joint decision to transition him from his current school. Now that Josie could walk to the secondary school opposite our house, a short, easy stroll, I had the freedom to drive Billy to a private school.

The smaller classes at the new school offered feelings of safety and reduced Billy's isolation, which was my primary hope. While the first term was a little bumpy and had its difficulties, including an incident involving him pushing another child (who, ironically, became his closest friend), Billy settled in by the second term. He formed new friendships and made steady progress. The immense relief I felt was a turning point, allowing me to release some of the constant worry that had weighed on me since our relocation. At last, Billy was thriving at school, and I could relax.

El describes finding a close friend at school as a source of comfort and as reducing loneliness. However, the underlying sense of not belonging persisted. She felt like she existed on the periphery of every group, able to mimic their behaviour just enough to take part in their activities. Despite her lack of conscious understanding, El experienced a constant feeling of isolation and loneliness.

She says, 'My new school was not merely a physical place. It was a place where I learned about societal expectations in young friendships. Friend groups divided themselves, with boys on one side and girls on the other, separated by an invisible wall. I gravitated towards the girls, their games and conversations resonating with me on a deeper level. But a powerful force held me back – the unspoken rules, the ingrained stereotypes. The fear of being ostracised, labelled a "sissy" for wanting to join the girls' playtime, became a heavy burden. So instead, I stayed within society's expected boundaries in those early years.'

While Billy adapted well to his new school over the next two years, the long-term financial burden of private secondary education, extending to sixth form, proved unsustainable for me as a single parent. Therefore, I embarked on the process of researching and applying to schools that I believed would offer the best fit and support for Billy.

4

TEENAGE TRANSITION

L ike most children navigating adolescence, Billy embarked on his own unique journey during his teenage years. He transitioned from his primary school to our local state-run boys' secondary school. I secured a place for him through the appeals process, hoping this new environment would allow Billy to continue his positive academic and social trajectory. I actively pursued the school, hoping it would offer Billy a place where he could form new friendships and explore new opportunities for personal and academic development.

However, after about a year, subtle shifts became evident. Billy, always an honest child, now seemed evasive and occasionally untruthful regarding schoolwork and friends. He retreated once again into the solace of his room, spending significant time engrossed in his Game Boy or Xbox. Online gaming filled his afternoons and most weekends, becoming his primary social interaction. While this wasn't ideal, I brushed aside my concerns, attributing his behaviour to the gaming culture prevalent among teenagers at that time. As a single parent, I had little time to butt heads with Billy on his social preferences, so I went with the flow.

While outbursts from Angry Billy became less frequent, a deeper sadness seemed to fester beneath the surface. The move to the new school and losing his old social circle had taken a toll. Billy experienced sleepless nights and a dwindling appetite. His new environment, devoid of the comfort of established friendships, I now realised, amplified his sense of isolation. Obliviously, I had chosen the wrong direction for Billy, causing his distress.

Seeking Answers

El says, 'I still grappled with feelings of not belonging, seeking refuge in online gaming's anonymity to explore unique identities and connect with others. However, solitude within my school environment also served a purpose – a space for self-discovery fuelled by a desire to understand my feelings of alienation.

'Driven by curiosity and need for solitude, I frequented the school library, researching the source of my discomfort. Stumbling upon the concept of body dysphoria, I discovered a term that resonated deeply with my lived experience. I delved into the topic, reading everything I could find about it, although I hadn't yet encountered the term transgender.

'Upon realising I might have body dysphoria, I embarked on a path of self-expression, attempting to embrace a more

traditionally masculine identity through sports, motor sports, and more traditional masculine pursuits. This approach, fuelled by fear of societal judgement and the observed mistreatment of a gay student at my all-boys school, led me to construct a facade. I would bury all feminine feelings and try to work from the 'guy' script I was given. However, the longer I maintained this inauthentic self, the deeper the loneliness and isolation became. Depression, anxiety, and feelings of hopelessness became unwelcome companions for me during these years.

'My heightened awareness of my vulnerability also translated into a strong protective instinct towards others facing bullying. While my intentions were rooted in empathy, I reacted to some situations by exceeding the necessary level, which led to the school taking disciplinary action because of my physically aggressive behaviour. My cycle of fear and overreaction intensified my struggles and further isolated me.

'I wasn't just sad; I was drowning in the murky depths of depression. The vibrant spark that once illuminated my eyes had dimmed, replaced by a hollowness that mirrored the despair I felt. Any attempt to fit in lay abandoned, the joy of learning superseded by a crushing indifference. Schoolwork, once a manageable challenge, became an insurmountable obstacle. The fog of depression clouded my concentration, making it difficult to focus or retain information. Sleep, instead of offering solace, became an escape, a refuge from the relentless feelings of negativity. Even the most basic tasks felt like wading through mud, the effort leaving me drained and dispirited. The insidious voice of depression whispered *its cruel message: "It doesn't matter what you do, El. You're going to be miserable, regardless."*

Unfortunately, in his bedroom, Billy kept all these emotions hidden from me – or maybe I just didn't have enough time to see them? Despite my efforts to review his homework and exam readiness, all he would say to my concerns was 'all OK.' Ultimately, Billy was now doing what was necessary to go unnoticed.

NAVIGATING POST-SECONDARY LIFE

illy's GCSE results, while lower than expected, still qualified him for further education. Regardless of my disappointment with his exam performance, I was determined to concentrate on finding a way forward. However, finding direction proved challenging for Billy. He seemed uncertain about his aspirations and embarked on several higher education courses, only to abandon them soon after, despite my efforts to persuade him otherwise.

Billy ultimately opted to leave full-time education and pursued various jobs. A six-month apprenticeship with a security company left him unfulfilled, leading him to seek other opportunities. Although care work offered some satisfaction, the long hours and low pay proved unsustainable. Despite various job trials, Billy remained lost on his career path. Confused and lacking enthusiasm, he resisted my attempts to motivate him to seek further education or specific job options.

His unhappiness was clear and deeply concerning; however, he remained silent about the underlying cause, even to me.

As I was a single parent during this period, I struggled with anger and frustration towards Billy's apparent lack of direction. My strong work ethic clashed with his situation, leading to frequent heated discussions that left the two of us feeling hurt and discouraged. It felt like walking on quicksand, trying to move forward without sinking again at every turn. Despite these challenges, we persevered together, united in our search for avenues that could offer Billy a sense of purpose and fulfilment.

A Turning Point

During a period of unemployment, Billy applied for and secured a spot on the Prince's Trust (now King's Trust) residential course, a programme designed for young adults that offers a blend of activities aimed at skill development, confidence building, social interaction, and ultimately employment opportunities. Billy's participation proved transformative, helping him establish positive routines and develop a plan to achieve his goals. While he engaged in fun and challenging group activities alongside learning key life and work skills – teamwork, leadership, and communication – Billy's confidence grew. The programme offered one-on-one support, aiding participants in navigating their next steps towards achieving their aspirations.

I hoped Billy would enjoy the experience, find connections with others, and thrive during the course. To my delight, when I picked him up, he introduced me to his first girlfriend.

Although it was a brief encounter, I was happy to meet her and witness his new-found sense of confidence and connection.

Later, after the course, a programme organiser informed me that Billy had flourished in his social interactions, forming strong friendships and showing unexpected leadership qualities. He rose to the challenge of leading his group, exceeding expectations and stepping outside his comfort zone. This experience fostered a sense of confidence and self-worth in Billy. Most noticeably, he discovered a capability for positive leadership, providing encouragement and compassion to his teammates – certainly, internal qualities that surprised even him.

Hearing these personal observations from Billy's team members swelled my pride. Of course, this positive assessment fuelled my hope that the programme had equipped him with the tools and confidence he needed to navigate his future.

Upon returning from the course, Billy exhibited a level of confidence I hadn't witnessed before. The programme's emphasis on teamwork and self-discovery had unveiled his inner strengths, courage, and personal beliefs. It undoubtedly contributed to his well-being, instilling positive habits and routines. Most importantly, the experience empowered Billy to embrace self-directed living, prioritising his own choices and values while navigating future challenges.

El's Authentic Evening at the Prince's Trust

During a Prince's Trust self-expression event where participants explored identity, El, who now privately identified as female, found a profoundly meaningful experience. Never before had she been able to present herself as feminine without judgement, a chance that brought immense comfort and personal validation.

Never before had El truly felt like she belonged. Gone were the days of awkward silences on the fringes of groups, replaced by a sense of belonging that transcended forced smiles and unanswered questions. Here, in this circle of acceptance, she was no longer an outsider yearning to be seen. She was in the centre, not just physically but emotionally. Conversations flowed effortlessly, punctuated by genuine laughter and shared experiences. This experience of being at the centre of a group, not just tolerated but embraced, was a turning point for El. It opened doors to a future where connection and belonging were not distant dreams but tangible reality.

Thank You

I would like to just take a moment to express my gratitude for the Prince's Trust and the enormous work they do with our young adults. The volunteers are amazing and dedicated to giving all participants a fantastic experience that will help them progress in their chosen paths. This course was a massive turning point for Billy and helped him to find himself and his purpose. Thank you!

Not long after his return home, Billy confided in me.

THE DAY EL SHARED HER TRUTH

'Mum, I wish to be seen as and recognised as a woman.' El's revelation was unexpected, and it overwhelmed me. I wrestled with a range of emotions including shock, disbelief, anger, sadness, and a deep sense of self-blame for not recognising her struggles sooner and not giving her the opportunity to seek my help earlier. My stomach tensed with fear and worry about El's future and that unwelcome but well-known feeling of shame.

It was a distressing turn of events. After navigating my initial shock, I grappled with my many emotions, attempting to stay calm and seek understanding through questions that, in hindsight, were insensitive and misinformed.

The situation appeared dreamlike and daunting. My initial responses, including the mention of 'girlfriends' and 'phases', and the comparison of my son's life experiences with potential future hardships, all stemmed from my poor understanding and awareness. Despite my best intentions, I failed to provide the support El needed. My poor grasp and lack of understanding about transgender experiences and identities prevented effective communication and hampered my good intentions. I was like a swan gliding on the water's surface, yet paddling furiously underneath, unsure how to navigate these waters.

I continued to babble on in my attempt to gain clarity, voicing concerns and questions that I now understand were insensitive and naive:

'Are you certain? Your life is going to be much harder, and people will discriminate against you. How do you know you want to change gender when you haven't even had a long-term girlfriend yet?'

My worries about potential future difficulties, such as discrimination, limited job prospects, and lack of social acceptance, I later realised, only highlighted how little I knew or understood about transgender issues and gender dysphoria. I was ignorance itself. None of those things, I now know, have any correlation to being trans.

In retrospect, I realise that my ingrained anxieties – my fear of losing control and my discomfort with uncertainty (two intense fears I had experienced since childhood) – manifested in my attempts to be supportive during my initial communication with El. I approached the situation from a place of great apprehension rather than with understanding – from fear rather than love. Unfortunately, this resulted in questions that were insensitive and lacked the empathy and knowledge that I should have shown towards El.

As a single mum, navigating these waters felt especially daunting. To make matters even more challenging, my then-boyfriend vehemently opposed my acceptance of El's revelation. Isolation and a strange sense of personal shame washed over me – shame that this was happening to *me*, not shame regarding my son. I am ashamed to say my initial reaction, fuelled by fear and uncertainty, was to focus on the impact this would have on my life – my family, my relationship, and potential disruptions. Of course, fear for my child's future and the challenges we might face together loomed large as well.

When El confided in me, I believed I was the first, but I learned later this wasn't the case. One of El's close friends played an essential part in supporting her journey.

El says, 'My initial hesitation and attempts to disclose my longing for transition to my mother stemmed from a fear of causing disappointment or negativity, not fear itself. The disclosure process itself, even to my best friend, was challenging for me, requiring multiple attempts, much stuttering, and careful wording before I could share my revelation.

'Fortunately, my friend's immediate and accepting response – "Thank God, El, I thought you were trying to tell me you were dying" – provided me with a significant boost of confidence. My friend's warm embrace and positive action convinced me that others close to me might react similarly.'

Even today, the gratitude I feel towards El's best friend for his compassionate response remains etched in my heart forever, as it influenced El's decision to trust me with her secret.

HINDSIGHT

After my initial shock, I was thankful for El's clarity and composure during our initial discussion. She had anticipated my confusion and distress and had proactively sought information from experts on transgender identity and affirmation. This enabled her to explain to me, clearly and calmly, her needs and her desired path to complete her journey. El stayed very calm, even when I clearly was not.

It's vital to recognise that our family's experience, while challenging, may not reflect the difficulties faced by many other families. Supporting a transgender child can heighten concerns, particularly when the child is young. While I struggled to accept El's identity, both at seventeen and beyond, I now understand the additional challenges faced by families with transgender children of a younger age.

Facing El's transition at seventeen was undeniably daunting. My anxiety around not knowing the 'right' path forward for her was a constant weight. Yet even amid my own anxieties, a profound realisation emerged. The fear experienced by parents of younger transgender children– those with kids as young as four, five, or seven – must be even more profound. The thought is indeed mind-blowing. Yet it's a reality for many families, and these parents need and deserve immense support and resources.

Unlike them, I didn't have to think about my child being refused entry into the girl's bathroom at school, other parents being upset or complaining, or verbal abuse in the corridors.

Even today, many transgender students face bullying and transphobic language at school, which often goes unreported. Our schools cannot always tackle these issues, along with other forms of bullying, violence, and social exclusion. Therefore, we must create safe and inclusive environments for all children, regardless of gender identity. Schools, in particular, have a crucial role to play in combating bullying, prejudice, and discrimination in all its forms.

In 1988, Margaret Thatcher's government passed Section 28, a legislative measure banning schools from promoting 'the teaching in mainstream schools of the acceptability of homosexuality as a family relationship':

Section 2 of the [1986 c. 10.] Local Government Act 1986 (prohibition of political publicity) – (1) A local authority shall not – (a) intentionally promote homosexuality or publish material with the intention of promoting homosexuality;

(b) promote the teaching in any maintained school of the acceptability of homosexuality as a pretended family relationship.

This led to teachers being unable to teach about LGBTQ+ issues or offer support to vulnerable individuals.

Although Section 28 was, thankfully, repealed in England and Wales in 2003, this legislation caused harm to teachings of this subject, pushing it back years, and led to a culture of silence that allowed prejudice among children and staff to persist far longer than it should have.

Government Guidance for Schools

In 2023, the UK government published *Gender Questioning Children: Non-Statutory Guidance for Schools and Colleges in England.* This document aims to provide schools with recommendations for creating inclusive environments for transgender students.

The guidance is not legally binding and has received mixed reactions. Some individuals believe it provides necessary support for transgender youth, while others express concerns about potential effects.

One specific point of contention is the use of the word *belief* regarding gender identity. This terminology differs from the established language used by the World Health Organisation, the UK census, and legal frameworks, which emphasise gender identity as an inherent characteristic rather than a belief.

The guidance encourages schools to consider the needs of the entire school community when supporting a transgender student's transition. However, it lacks specific criteria for determining the threshold of 'reasonable impact' that would justify a school refusing a student's request for social transition within the school environment.

It also advises against flexibility in school uniform policies, although this specific recommendation is subject to ongoing discussions.

Ultimately, the responsibility of implementing the guidance falls on individual schools. Regardless of the approach adopted by each school, it's vital to acknowledge that varying viewpoints may exist within the school community.

The government is currently seeking input from parents and teachers (but not young trans children) regarding this guidance.

As a supply teacher since 2019, I've observed both signs of progress and areas requiring further improvement regarding LGBTQ+ inclusion in schools. While instances of bullying and discriminatory language may not be prominent in every classroom or playground, their continuing occurrence is unacceptable and demands ongoing efforts towards creating safe and inclusive environments.

Every child deserves equal treatment, regardless of their race, gender identity, sexual orientation, or ability. It's harmful to perpetuate a narrative that any child needs protection from another child's identity. Our priority should be to create safe and supportive school environments that ensure the protection of all children from harassment or harm.

True freedom of expression allows children to explore their individuality, experiment with their appearance, and express themselves authentically. Such a supportive environment fosters belonging and acceptance, benefiting everyone.

Fear and misinformation contribute to prejudice and discrimination. To create a supportive and inclusive environment, it's crucial that we educate ourselves – staff, students, and parents alike. We should prioritise listening to transgender individuals, their loved ones, and those familiar with transgender experiences. Their lived realities and insights are invaluable for dispelling misconceptions and fostering greater understanding.

El's decision to maintain privacy during her school years shielded me from any school-related issues. El's experience raises interesting questions about balancing privacy with navigating the world as a transgender individual. While her decision to remain private during school years meant a smoother journey for me, it also highlights the challenges transgender students face within the current education system.

Under the Equality Act, single-sex schools can refuse admission to students who don't identify with the gender assigned to them at birth. This creates an additional hurdle for transgender youths seeking an education in an environment that best suits them. This stance on admissions in single-sex schools sparks a conversation about inclusivity and the right learning environment for all students. Maybe we should consider a more thoughtful approach that considers a student's gender identity beyond their assigned birth sex.

While my journey may not encompass the full spectrum of experiences faced by parents of transgender children, I continue to learn and grow in my understanding. I have immense respect and admiration for those parents and caregivers who provide unwavering support to young people exploring their gender identity. Your strength, courage, and love are inspiring.

8

BEGINNING THE JOURNEY

When El first disclosed her identity, I confess I had little knowledge and understanding of transgender experiences. While I knew about the increasing visibility of transgender individuals in society, my personal exposure remained limited. Despite a growing presence on television, in magazines, and on social media, my awareness was limited.

This ignorance influenced my initial response. Feeling overwhelmed and unsure of how to support El, I suggested seeking counselling, hoping it would address her feelings about her gender identity. (Secretly, I hoped it would change her mind.) I then dismissed her identity as a passing phase – a way to minimise my worry. This approach, rooted in misinformation, astonishment, and fear, was misguided.

However, my conviction remains unwavering that sending El to counselling at that stage was beneficial. Looking back, counselling may have served multiple purposes. Perhaps it provided El with a safe space to explore her identity while allowing me some space to grapple with my understanding. In hindsight, I suspect it was mainly the latter.

We had the good fortune to find a qualified therapist specialising in gender identity, and El agreed to attend, if only to appease me. She attended individual sessions biweekly, allowing her to explore her journey and receive support in a safe and confidential space. While respecting her privacy, I expressed an interest in her progress and encouraged her to share her experience if she wished. Her responses were brief, often just a simple 'Yep, it went okay.' I'd respond with a forced 'that's great' and tuck my worry and anxiety back into that mental box.

At my request, El continued with counselling for six months. Afterward, I had to concede that El's transition was indeed going to happen. Her unwavering determination clarified that transitioning formed an integral part of her identity, and denying her that truth was unsustainable. Her argument was emotional and compelling. I faced a choice: get on board or lose contact with my child. Facing the prospect of losing contact with El if I defied her (she wasn't yet quite eighteen) motivated me to seek support and understanding. I had to understand El's journey.

The memory of that defiant two-year-old standing on the sand with jaw jutting out, refusing to enter the sea, was a poignant reminder. Even at that young age, El possessed an undeniable determination. El, like that child eventually drawn to the cool embrace of the sea, would conquer her fears and forge her own path. My role, I realised, wasn't to force her into the water but to be a constant presence, a provider of unwavering support. Just as I had offered a gentle hand to that hesitant child, guiding her towards the ocean's gentleness, I would again need to be there for El. Yet I had no clue how to navigate these waters, which promised to be choppy!

Transgender individuals decide to navigate their journeys in various ways and at their own pace. Some may choose privacy or gradual disclosure, while others may engage more publicly with the LGBTQ+ community. El, at that stage, chose a private path, and I respected her decision to lead the way, so we didn't attend local transgender groups, although they were recommended to us.

During this time, I became strongly aware of persistent misconceptions regarding the motivations behind transgender individuals' desire to transition. Many of these concerns troubled me. Some argue that young people are influenced by their peers to transition; they claim it is a 'social contagion'. Others believe online influencers glorify medical transition, causing impressionable youths to follow suit. Still others suggest young adults transition to 'fit in' or be popular at schools, or even to follow what they believe is a cool trend.

Like other forms of identity, transgender identity arises from a complex interplay of factors. Genetics, environment, cultural influences, and individual experiences likely all contribute to creating gender identity. Unfortunately, there's currently limited conclusive evidence to pinpoint the exact causes.

There may be limitations to our current understanding of this topic – there certainly were to mine at this time – but I must emphasise the crucial role of accurate information in combating harmful stereotypes and creating supportive environments for transgender individuals.

The significant mental and emotional challenges faced by many transgender youths contradict the idea that they're seeking attention or trying to be 'interesting'. My experience suggests that many young trans people would, if possible, choose to navigate their transition privately.

The journey of any transgender person is deeply personal and focused on self-discovery and authenticity. Certainly, if El could have completed her journey with no one knowing, she would have chosen that option. El's transition was about her own gender identity; external factors or influences did not motivate it.

Some of my family members also questioned the motivation behind El's gender identity, not understanding the complexity of such experiences.

Whether I concurred with any of these concerns became insignificant: as of July 2014, El turned eighteen. She was an adult and could now forge her own path.

NAVIGATING PERSONAL
INSECURITIES

As El transitioned into adulthood, she sought greater independence, including making her own healthcare decisions. Respecting El's privacy and in line with patient confidentiality guidelines, I had limited direct involvement with her healthcare providers. El's growing independence, while positive, brought up new emotions for me. As someone who valued control and predictability, dealing with this change proved challenging.

I'd always prioritised control in my life and decisions, and I'd wanted to ensure stability and security for my children. Surrendering control wasn't easy. For me, it required a fundamental shift in perspective.

The truth, uncomfortable as it may have been to admit, showed me that my desire for control extended beyond mere order and stability. Control served as a shield against a multitude of fears: the fear of failing my children, the fear of the unknown, and a deep-seated fear of judgement that stemmed from my childhood. I held on to control like I was clutching a life raft in a turbulent sea, even if it entailed suppressing the very individuals I was attempting to safeguard. I was now losing this control.

Giving up control wasn't a direct journey for me. There were detours, sharp turns, and moments where frustration bubbled over. It was tough to be absent from El's assessments and GP meetings, and it was even harder not to help El. There were many moments when I found it difficult to adapt to this new chapter in my relationship with El. But through open communication, we navigated the uncharted waters together. One tearful night, I confessed my anxieties, including the fear of not being the parent El needed. El, with a maturity that belied her years, squeezed my hand. 'We'll figure it out together,' she whispered.

ACCESSING GENDER-AFFIRMING SERVICES IN THE UK

I t was always El's intention to pursue both social and medical transitioning, and she actively sought options available to her as she began her journey.

Gender transition is a multifaceted journey, unique to each individual. Some individuals may begin this journey by expressing their preferred gender in a safe and supportive environment. Over time, they may integrate changes in multiple aspects of their lives, including the following:

- **Appearance**: They may adopt clothing styles, grooming habits, and hairstyles associated with their affirmed gender.
- **Identity**: They may choose a new name and, if possible, update gender markers on legal documents.
- **Medical Interventions**: Some individuals may pursue hormone therapy or gender-affirming surgeries to align their physical body with their gender identity.

There is no single 'right' way to transition. Each individual's choices and journey are profoundly intimate and deserve respect.

In the UK, those seeking gender identity–related support can access services through their GP. This initial step allows for personalised guidance and exploration of options.

Another potential referral option is a specialised gender identity clinic. These clinics offer assessment, support, and treatment for people experiencing gender dysphoria. While some individuals choose medical transition (hormone therapy or surgery) as part of their journey, it's essential to remember that this is a choice. Not everyone elects to pursue medical transition. Many factors influence an individual's decisions regarding transition, including safety considerations, financial feasibility, personal preferences, and access to resources.

While GPs play a critical role in providing initial support and guidance, their training in transgender healthcare has recognised gaps. This led to detrimental experiences for El as she sought support. El constantly had to repeat requests because of the revolving door of staff members answering the phone and the obstacles to direct contact with her GP. Many staff members answering the phone were not even aware of whether the service El required, specifically blood tests to continue her hormone treatment, was available and often had to find out, or they just flatly refused her the service.

El's initial journey also involved navigating various assessments to ascertain her options. The journey, characterised as a marathon rather than a sprint, was not a simple task. The endless assessments, with a revolving door of professionals asking the same questions, took a toll on El. Each session chipped away at her sense of self. 'Am I just a collection of symptoms?' she would groan. Witnessing her struggle time and time again after each one was heartbreaking. The repetitive nature of the assessments became a point of contention for El.

El says, 'While I comprehended the purpose of these assessments, I felt that my identity was consistently being questioned, with restricted chances for genuine conversation or recognition of my perspective. Repeated inquiries about family dynamics, while relevant, caused me unnecessary distress because of their private nature and frequent repetition. The very act of being assessed felt invalidating to me. The essence of my lived experiences seemed to disappear in a maze of clinical terms and checklists.'

El's first GP appointment didn't go smoothly. The doctor didn't seem informed about her transition journey, and the communication style came across as unsupportive. El felt that the doctor did not acknowledge her needs, and the general approach was dismissive. She felt the GP was almost aggressively trying to change her mind. Tears welled up in her eyes as she recounted the doctor's dismissive tone, the constant interruptions, and the barrage of ill-informed questions. Phrases like 'just a phase' and questions such as 'Are you sure about this?' were all too often involved. This wasn't meant to be a fight. The experience left a deep scar, a gnawing distrust of a system that was supposed to provide her support.

For me, the difficulty lay in observing El's distress during the assessments. She'd return home, shoulders slumped, a tremor in her voice as she recounted the endless questions and the clinical indifference. My sole course of action was to sit there as the weight of her frustration filled the air and simply listen. Exhaustion and frustration would etch El's face after those appointments. My stomach would clench, a helpless ache mirroring hers. Sometimes all I could manage was to pull her close and hold her, overwhelmed by a deep sense of powerlessness.

El's disheartening experience at the very beginning of her journey with her GP became a catalyst for change for us. Together, we began a mission to find a doctor who celebrated El's identity instead of challenging it. LGBTQ+ organisations provided invaluable resources, and recommendations from friends pointed us in the right direction. Finally, we found her – a doctor who acknowledged El's perspective, answered her questions with respect, and outlined a clear path forward. Part of that straightforward way for El was to register with the closest NHS gender clinic.

Initially happy and excited to register at the clinic, El experienced immense frustration because of the prolonged waiting times. The agonising waits, with weeks bleeding into months, weren't just a test of patience; they meant constant missed opportunities to get hormone treatment and begin her transition.

El's mounting anxiety and emotional struggles sometimes manifested in her missing clinic appointments. The initial consultation, a lifeline thrown to her amid uncertainty, seemed to recede further with every missed appointment or cancellation from the clinic. She dreaded losing her place in line for treatment, and this was compounded by the burden of rescheduling months in advance. Unfortunately, because of limited resources, the NHS gender clinic system had limited availability for rescheduling appointments, and the combination of El's work obligations with limited responsiveness from the clinic created further difficulties. This all fuelled a vicious cycle of despair for El, which continued to affect her mental health.

This constant cycle of missed appointments and delays in obtaining hormones spiralled El into a vortex of despair, driven by the fear of losing progress or jeopardising her transition. The constant battles to get the support she needed were exhausting. It was a constant merry-go-round. The fragile hope she had clung to at the beginning, the belief that she could navigate her way to happiness with support from professionals, shattered into a million pieces. This crushing blow, on top of the existing weight of depression, left El feeling more isolated and hopeless than ever before. It was the catalyst that propelled her into a destructive cycle of self-harm. El would intentionally cut her arms in discreet areas that would be concealed by clothing.

El's experience was not unique then and is commonplace today. It's a harsh reality that persists for many transitioners with lengthy waiting times and inexperienced or limited specialists. A more compassionate and adaptable system, with extended hours, virtual consultations, and a recognition of the unique challenges faced by transgender individuals, would be a crucial step towards a fairer healthcare experience.

El says, 'My journey wasn't just about navigating a healthcare system; it was a fight against feeling being trapped in a system designed to delay, not expedite, my progress.'

PRIVATE OPTIONS

Seeking a more streamlined and compassionate approach, El refused to give up. Her resourceful spirit (or should I say undeniable determination) ignited once again, and she set off on a quest for alternative options. Through this research and with the help of her original therapist, she discovered GenderGP.

El pursued transitioning through GenderGP private healthcare because of the lengthy waiting times within the public healthcare system. Although going private came at a significant personal cost, it enabled her to begin hormone therapy much sooner. Finding affordable resources, such as counselling, hormone therapy, medical procedures, and the necessary social support, had been fraught with delays and obstacles.

El had been facing at least two years from first seeing her GP to starting medical transitioning hormones via the NHS and their gender clinic (and that was before Covid!). For those who want to transition quicker, the only option is to get hormones privately via services offered by GenderGP or similar private practices.

This was not inexpensive, and on top of this came laser treatment for hair removal, specialised make-up, and clothing (especially shoes) that were suitable and desirable for El to wear.

The NHS waiting lists for specific procedures, such as laser treatment, necessitated seeking further private alternatives. The waiting list for hair removal was lengthy, and the NHS did not provide enough sessions. This was an area of massive discomfort for El, who'd had strong, dark facial hair since puberty, so we again went private. To date, she has completed over twenty hour-long sessions, and counting.

GenderGP

The private practice El used, GenderGP, offers a range of services to assist transgender individuals on their journeys. These services include advocacy, support, advice, healthcare, and access to additional resources.

El used GenderGP's services to request prescriptions, treatment reviews, blood tests, and surgical referrals. She is also now using their support to change her gender marker on legal documents.

GenderGP charges an initial fee, and they offer payment plans and subscriptions. If you're a parent of a transgender child, they can offer advice to you, your child, and your doctor if you wish.

Once El had registered with GenderGP, she found herself in a supportive environment specifically designed to help her. A gender specialist met with El every six months to review her progress, get updates on her current situation, and assist with any issues she might go through. They were available to El whenever she needed them for advice, counselling, or even just a calming, encouraging ear. El now felt she was making progress on her journey. This also enabled me to sit on the sidelines to some degree, which I did.

It helps if a patient's regular doctor will prescribe for them when they are under GenderGP's supervision. If your child's GP will allow this, GenderGP will send that GP a treatment summary advising them what treatment options to follow.

If that option isn't available, then GenderGP can issue a private prescription, and you can purchase your medication privately. El chose this option.

Despite this, El still needed to use her GP. Securing timely blood tests through the local GP surgery to receive and continue her hormone treatment via GenderGP often proved to be a frustrating and challenging experience for El during the initial stages of her transitioning. Not equipped or experienced in managing transgender healthcare, the GP surgery did not have the resources or guidance to handle this process efficiently. On one occasion, they refused to do a blood test for El because she had opted to go private for her gender identity treatment. She had to fight this decision and did so successfully.

The NHS, though well-intentioned, often fell short. Limited appointments outside El's working hours created a domino effect. Missing a blood test meant delays in hormone therapy, affecting El's physical and emotional well-being. Her frustration was palpable. The NHS, a system designed to provide healthcare, often created barriers to it.

El had no choice but to push through these challenges, persistently advocating for her needs and finding solutions to overcome the all too frequent obstacles presented by the limitations of the NHS. The journey was far from smooth, but with perseverance and resourcefulness, El navigated the roadblocks, her determination and resilience once again paving the way with the support of GenderGP.

Once El was receiving hormone treatment, GenderGP requested blood test results for testosterone (every three months) and oestrogen (every three months), as well as a full health check (every year).

They also adjusted the timings and frequency of these tests based on any changes throughout the journey or results they got.

In order to get continuous referrals, El had to meet established guidelines, including living in her identified gender role for at least twelve months and participating in specialised counselling to assess and monitor her mental health during her transition journey. El did this specialised counselling through GenderGP.

Because El constantly faced difficulties and delays in obtaining documentation from her GP, she ended up receiving all her medical surgery referrals through GenderGP.

Her journey, though arduous, serves as a reminder of the value of perseverance. If you or someone you know is facing similar challenges, know that you're not alone. Explore online resources, connect with local LGBTQ+ organisations, and raise your voice for change. There are other avenues for supporting your child's transitioning beyond the usual GP and NHS gender clinic – although I am sad to say they are all private.

As I witnessed El's meticulous research, the detailed timeline she crafted for her transition journey ignited a bittersweet cocktail of emotions within me. Pride, a fierce and unwavering one, swelled in my chest. El, my child, was taking charge of her life, navigating this uncharted territory with courage and determination. But alongside my pride came a gnawing sense of inadequacy. Here I was, the parent, supposed to be the guide, yet El had become the trailblazer. Guilt, a serpent coiling around my heart, threatened to suffocate my pride. I knew I was still living in avoidance mode.

Despite my anxieties, I knew supporting El was my role. This meant diving head first into a world I knew little about. Navigating the vast landscape of transgender experiences proved challenging. Reliable information felt elusive. New vocabulary swirled around me, threatening to overwhelm. Confronting my unconscious biases, however uncomfortable, was an essential part of the process. The initial meeting with El's therapist, though not a magic bullet, served as a starting point. Determined to understand El's journey, I persisted, fuelled by love and a commitment to growth. But I knew I still had many personal hurdles to overcome.

12

UNCERTAINTY AND DOUBT

Josie, El's sister, had already left home for university when El began transitioning, which provided some distance for her from the initial challenges and uncertainty that we both were experiencing. While aiming to protect Josie from potential distress and recognising the intricacies of all our emotions at this time, I sought ways to manage the impact on her to the best of my ability. I tried to be positive with Josie when discussing El and her progress, bottling up my concerns and worries as much as possible. In fact, on reflection, I did this frequently, with many of those around me.

El's transition triggered a wave of self-doubt and unfamiliar emotions within me. A flurry of anxious thoughts spiralled through my mind. Many centred on blame. Was I selfish to have left her father, depriving El of a balanced upbringing with both male and female role models? I wondered. Had

I inadvertently influenced El's identity through my shared activities with Josie, making her feel I loved Josie more?

Josie and I would do 'girly' things like clothes shopping, hair, and make-up, often spending quality time together. Fear gnawed at me. Had I unknowingly pushed El away?

External anxieties fuelled the internal fire. I worried people would think this was my fault. The rise in people expressing issues with their birth gender struck me as significant, feeding my fear that *transgender* was just a trendy label El had adopted online in search of belonging.

I questioned my parenting choices, wondering if I had somehow steered El's identity in the wrong direction. *She's unhappy, I know that,* I thought, *but will this path lead to happiness? Who will accept her, understand her, love her? What if it doesn't work out? What if this is a mistake?* This single paralysing fear threatened to annihilate me.

In one desperate moment, I uttered the unthinkable. I made the terrible mistake of comparing El's situation to a terminal illness. The words were insensitive and caused her immense pain. I regret my actions and the devastation they caused El.

El shared that this comparison, particularly coming from someone she loved and trusted, was especially devastating. While she might have received worse insults during her transition, the emotional impact of these words coming from her mother was more profound.

I regret this hurtful statement I made to El and acknowledge the harmful impact my words had on her. The emotional turmoil I was experiencing doesn't excuse my words or diminish their impact.

El's understanding and forgiveness are a testament to her strength and compassion. Despite the limitations of my knowledge and understanding, I am incredibly grateful for her continued willingness to confide in me throughout her journey.

She constantly forgave me for my ignorance, limiting beliefs, and, at times, selfish actions and words. Today, El also forgives me with a smile on her face for the odd pronoun slip.

Billy and I in 2013, the last summer before Billy confided in me and started his transition.

THE WEDDING

Together, El and I embarked on a journey to understand the challenges of adult gender transition in the UK. As we moved forward together, we encountered an absence of clear and readily available information, necessitating a step-by-step approach to navigating the process. Without a pre-existing blueprint, I relied on my love and commitment to support El in the best way I could.

We also had some personal, heartfelt, and thought-provoking discussions, mainly about children. While I expressed a personal desire for grandchildren, I acknowledged and respected El's decision not to have any. I felt a profound sadness at this news. My hope for El was a different life. I knew she would have made a fabulous parent, and I didn't want her to grow old alone or miss out on the joy of parenthood.

'Why not freeze sperm just in case?' I pleaded. 'You might meet someone one day and change your mind.'

El, ever thoughtful, had a clear perspective on this. She had considered the topic of children and made her decision. While I processed my own emotions, we continued our journey together.

El also shared the heart-warming story behind her chosen name. It embodied elements dear to each of us. She'd chosen the name I had envisioned for her if she had been born a girl, and a middle name that paid tribute to her beloved grandmother.

The next step involved informing El's father, whom I had separated from years ago. Though we maintained a cordial relationship, his approach to El's transition differed from mine. While his initial lack of engagement created feelings of isolation, she and I continued to support each other throughout her journey.

El's father lived five hours away, limiting his ability to witness El's daily experiences during her transition. The physical distance also made it difficult for them to have regular in-person interactions. This geographical distance, along with the complexities of El's journey, presented unique challenges in their communication and understanding.

In conversations, El's father initially expressed support for El. While he chose not to openly discuss the matter with others, I acknowledged his approach, which I suspected was influenced by various personal factors. However, one decision I disagreed with was her father's conditions for El's attending her stepsister's wedding.

This situation presented a distinct challenge for El, as the invitation was contingent on her presenting in a way that did not align with her gender identity, as her father had not told El's stepsister about her transitioning.

El took her father's comments to heart, feeling that he didn't acknowledge the significance of her attending the event authentically. She felt her father was implying that she craved attention and wanted the spotlight. His statement made El feel hurt and excluded. Doubt ravaged her. Was her wish to go as El selfish?

Nevertheless, El attended the wedding in Cornwall, accompanied by her sister, Josie. Following their father's request, El presented as male and maintained confidentiality.

El says, 'During the day, I had to stand outside for a picture with my sister, Josie. Someone commented on how handsome I was. The word handsome *hung in the air, a cruel irony. For me, it wasn't a compliment; it was a rejection, a denial of my true self. The word belonged to a world I was desperately trying to leave behind, a world that defined me by my masculinity and not by who I truly was. I wondered, Would they ever see me as El? Would I always feel trapped in the perception of others as a man in a girl's body, constantly struggling with confusion and discomfort? It was not a positive moment.*

'The groom also commented about my hair. I had grown it longer before the wedding. "What are you, a girl?" he said. It was supposed to be funny, a harmless jab. But for me, it was like a punch to the gut, an insensitive remark. The groom did not know, of course, of the journey I had taken, the courage it took to embrace my identity. A knot of frustration tightened in my stomach. Should I correct him, risk upsetting my father and

receiving unwanted attention? Or should I swallow my feelings and remain invisible, a strategy that was chipping away at my spirit?

'The wedding reception was like a pressure cooker, the forced merriment suffocating me. I tried to hold it together, a smile plastered on my face as I exchanged pleasantries with distant relatives. But beneath the facade, a storm was brewing. Finally, I couldn't take it anymore. The need for air, a desperate gasp for escape, propelled me towards the exit.

'My father's anger, clear to see, accused me of ruining the evening. However, I couldn't hear the words over the roar of my own emotions. I wished I could explain, but I needed to escape. Perhaps, I thought later, if there had been a moment of quiet understanding, a chance to communicate my distress, things could have been different.'

What was supposed to be a step forward for El became a cruel reminder of the hurdles she faced. As El returned home, her emotional turmoil was palpable, a stark contrast to the hopeful spirit she possessed before leaving for Cornwall. Raw emotions, a tangle of hurt and frustration, lingered with the rift between El and her father. Witnessing her pain ignited a fire of anger within me. The very people entrusted with El's well-being had disregarded her authenticity, causing her immense pain and distress. I was not happy.

RESEARCH

El's distress upon returning from Cornwall highlighted the gaps in my understanding of transgender identities and experiences. I committed myself to learning and gathering information so I could better support her.

In my initial search for answers, I encountered one statistic suggesting that over 80 percent of transgender children desist from transitioning – in other words, they re-identify with the gender assigned to them at birth before receiving any medical intervention. Unfortunately, I couldn't assess its credibility, but I kept this 'gem of information' in the recesses of my memory.

Recognising the value of ongoing education, I pursued knowledge about various identities within the LGBTQ+ spectrum, including asexuality, bisexuality, pansexuality, non-binary identities, and more. This began a long, continuous learning journey for me that was instrumental in my ability to effectively support El.

Witnessing El's ongoing emotional struggles with anxiety and depression during this time was painful. It underscored the need for active listening and support from me, prompting me to abandon any hesitation and engage in this journey alongside El.

I realised I needed to stop tiptoeing around this issue. I took my head out of the sand (or, as some might say, my backside) and, taking responsibility for my initial avoidance, I sought education on transgender experiences, medical options, and available financial help.

My research often exposed me to harmful and discriminatory attitudes toward transgender individuals. These negative portrayals only heightened my concerns for El's welfare and future safety.

Coming to terms with El's experience was an emotional process filled with uncertainty, fear, and worry. While I had difficulty, I gradually reached a point of partial acceptance and started openly communicating with close friends. While some were supportive and others curious, most really didn't have a clue about what *transgender* or *body dysphoria* meant. I understood and accepted this. After all, I had only begun to understand it myself.

Intending to offer support, loved ones inadvertently relied on outdated information or personal opinions. The comments, though well meant, missed the mark by emphasising interests or behaviours that El considered unrelated to her identity.

Friends and family chipped in with their thoughts too: 'But he's into gaming', 'He doesn't like clothes shopping', 'It's a phase and will pass.' (*Yes, please!* I thought.)

Sharing the news with Josie, who is close to El, was an emotional moment for us all.

The weight of the news pressed down on both of us; Josie struggled to understand my own frantic search for answers.

Any sense of being out of control, a constant shadow throughout my life, had always triggered a complex mix of emotions and a feeling of unease in me. Meticulous planning, control over my environment, and a rigid schedule and routine were the threads I wove into my comfort blanket. I craved certainty in my life and had worked hard to get it, but the situation in which I now found myself was ripping away my comfort blanket, leaving fear in its wake.

15

CURIOSITY AND INTRIGUE

For many, the term *trans* represents an unfamiliar concept. Over time, I've encountered various responses from friends, family, and colleagues as they grappled with their understanding of transgender identities and El's transition. It's important to remember these responses are individual and don't reflect the views of entire groups.

When those close to her first learned about El's journey, I often encountered questions about her transition process, starting with inquiries about medical interventions or public restroom facilities. While I initially shared similar curiosities, I came to understand that these questions, though stemming from genuine curiosity or lack of awareness, could be intrusive.

The legal landscape surrounding gender identity and public facilities varies across countries. In the UK, individuals may use facilities aligned with their gender identity, while some states in the US base access on birth certificates. Much controversy remains about the acceptance of trans women in female-only spaces, such as toilets, domestic abuse refuges, and prisons. It's important to consult reliable sources for accurate legal information specific to your location.

These inquiries about specific stages of her transition journey caused El understandable discomfort. Questions were often intrusive and placed an unnecessary focus on medical details. In their curiosity, many forgot to respect El's privacy. El, like everyone, should have her right to privacy upheld, and we should remember that no one must disclose personal medical information, however interested anyone may be.

It's also beneficial to recognise the difference between gender identity and sexual orientation. While both are aspects of personal identity, they are distinct concepts. Gender identity is a person's internal sense of being male, female, or something else, while sexual orientation is the romantic or sexual attraction they have towards others.

Understanding Sexual Orientation

Sexual orientation refers to who a person is attracted to romantically, emotionally, and sexually. It describes who you want to be with, not who you are.

People experience sexual orientation in diverse ways:

Same-sex attraction refers to individuals who are attracted to people of the same gender. Terms such as *gay*, *lesbian*, or *homosexual* may be used by these people to describe their sexual orientation.

Bisexuality is used to describe an attraction to both men and women.

Pansexuality or *queer* may be used to describe attraction to individuals across a diverse range of gender identities.

Asexuality is used to describe individuals who experience no sexual attraction to anyone.

Questioning and *curious* are used to describe individuals who are unsure about their sexual orientation.

I am not sure I've ever agreed with the concept of labelling ourselves or each other, and some people may feel that they don't exactly fit or want to fit into any labelled identity. It's up to each of us to decide how to label ourselves, if at all. Not everyone feels that labels are the most helpful way to understand their experiences.

Labels are a choice. Individuals may decide how they identify and whether they use labels at all.

Labels can be fluid. A person's identity and understanding of themselves can develop over time, and their chosen labels might change as well.

Labels are not exclusive. Some individuals may find multiple labels resonate with them, while others may prefer no labels at all.

Unfortunately, El's journey involved encountering negative and uninformed opinions. Some individuals, often lacking understanding of transgender identities, expressed the following assumptions about El, which many other transgender people encounter:

She was an attention-seeker. This harmful misconception is rooted in prejudice and disregards the personal struggles and complexities of transgender individuals.

She was confused because of the absence of a male role model. This stereotype perpetuates harmful and outdated views on gender identity and family dynamics. Gender identity is not affected by the presence or absence of specific gender roles in one's life.

A good deal of literature and online sources claim that certain transgender children choose to transition because they have an assertive mother or grew up without a father. There is absolutely no verified evidence to uphold this position. The evidence that body dysphoria is an innate condition, unrelated to upbringing, is convincing. The origins of the hurtful opinions I faced regarding El's transitioning were sometimes unclear, and without a doubt, some of these opinions were unhelpful.

The media coverage at this time was further complicated by the involvement of celebrities who, despite not being transgender themselves, felt compelled to share their opinions on transgender identities. Comedians who relied on jokes about their genitals often targeted transgender people. A joke should strive to be entertaining rather than offensive. That's what makes it funny. Anything else stems from an absence of respect rather than genuine humour and can sometimes seem no more elevated than online trolling. There is a distinction between making a light-hearted joke about the transgender community and making a derogatory comment about it.

Media coverage did sometimes provide me with insight into gender identity, but it was often uninformed and perpetuated harmful myths about the causes of transgender identity, such as family dynamics. Scientific evidence does not support these assertions. The superstition that solo mothers cause gender dysphoria always felt personal and hurtful to me – as harmful as the discredited theory that 'refrigerator mothers' cause autism.

I had to remind myself to seek reliable information from reputable LGBTQ+ organisations rather than succumbing to societal pressures or seeking explanations from inaccurate online sources. I refrained from reading alarmist headlines on the increasing number of people disclosing their gender identity on the news or listening to people's ill-informed ideas on transgender issues. Attributing blame or assuming fault where there might not be any would only hinder my journey of understanding and acceptance.

I confess that the number of individuals coming forward about their gender identity did initially worry me, but I discovered that this increase didn't reflect an actual increase in the prevalence of transgender individuals, as suggested by the media, but greater societal acceptance and visibility.

Body dysphoria, I understood, is a complex experience that varies among individuals. While some studies suggest a biological component, the exact cause remains unknown. It's crucial to focus on understanding and supporting individuals experiencing dysphoria, rather than perpetuating myths about its origins.

In 2014, at the beginning of El's journey, support groups and avenues of support for parents of transgender children in the UK were not as available as in the US. While some resources existed, I wasn't aware of them.

Despite my internal fear and reservations, I silently rooted for El and tried to provide support, but sharing our journey only with a select few limited my opportunities for broader understanding and personal growth. My own emotional processing was inadequate, as I harboured the unconscious hope that El would eventually change her mind. This affected my willingness to seek any kind of external support, although I was determined to educate myself.

Avoiding conflict with El, though the right decision, masked my internal struggles, which were rooted in fear and negativity. These struggles often manifested in my actions. This gap between my outward support and inner turmoil undoubtedly affected El. My subconscious resistance to accepting the situation was at odds with my expressed support and true understanding.

Subconscious fears can manifest in unforeseen ways, sometimes revealing hidden biases. This became clear when I made judgements and assessments without engaging in conscious thought. I also had recurring dreams that may have represented underlying anxieties.

In one recurring dream, I would be fast asleep when suddenly, there was a knock on the door. I would run down the stairs and see through the glass door the outline of two people. It was the police standing outside my door.

In a blind panic, I'd fling open the door and shout, 'Please do not let this be about Josie!'

I often woke from this dream in a state of panic, sweating and crying. It seemed to me that my dream was telling me that I'd subconsciously chosen between my two children. It was like one of those quandaries in which a mother is forced to save only one of her two drowning children, and the dream was telling me I'd chosen Josie. In reality, of course, that wasn't true: I could never have chosen between my children, both of whom I loved dearly. Perhaps my dream was an expression of my anxiety about being unable to deal with a double burden: Billy's situation was almost more than I could deal with on its own, and I was afraid the pain would cripple me if I lost Josie as well. Still, the dream triggered overwhelming feelings of shame and guilt, causing me significant emotional distress – all of which remain when I recall that dream today.

16

FRIENDS

El found unwavering support from her long-term friends. Regardless of her gender identity, they embraced her journey and valued her friendship. From their seamless integration of El's preferred pronouns into conversations to accompanying her to appointments and offering a shoulder to cry on, their actions spoke volumes. Game nights remained a cherished tradition. Movie marathons transformed into discussions on representation and identity. Their friendship, a testament to the power of acceptance, developed alongside El.

They embraced new experiences, and sharing secrets added another layer to their already strong bond. El's friends became not just her support system but her cheerleaders, celebrating her journey while cherishing the core of who she was. Her friends became a haven, a safe space where she could shed any anxieties and be herself.

Witnessing their effortless acceptance challenged my own preconceived notions about friendship. Through their unwavering support, they became my teachers as well. True friendship, I came to understand, transcends labels and societal expectations.

El made new friends too. A chance meeting on one fun-filled evening held the promise of something more, a connection that would resonate throughout El's life, though its exact significance then remained a beautiful mystery.

El's transition also coincided with the loss of some friendships, which was painful for her. The social dynamics inherent in an all-boys school environment can be challenging, and it's possible that some former friends felt unsure about how to navigate this significant change. While some appeared accepting, the connections gradually faded, and others severed communication entirely. El, with remarkable strength, acknowledged these losses and continued moving forward on her journey.

17

FAMILY

El's journey not only brought personal challenges for me but also affected family dynamics. El began expressing herself through various personal choices, including changing her clothing style and pronouns, adopting the name El, and starting hormonal therapy. I used El's chosen name while initially struggling with pronouns. My mother, despite her best efforts, found it challenging to remember El's name, and pronouns proved difficult for her to adopt.

While my family members attempted to be understanding, navigating unfamiliar territory involved some struggles. This resulted in my declining to attend family events because I felt El and I were being scrutinised or judged.

These feelings may have stemmed from my personal anxieties and insecurities about being a spectacle to others. While certain comments from family, like 'He has always been different, hasn't he?' were insensitive and hurtful, they likely originated from a lack of understanding rather than malicious intent.

Although my family's support was imperfect, it was more than many have. Still, the lack of complete understanding and muted conversation contributed to feelings of isolation, sadness, and personal hurt for El and me.

El's journey also exposed cracks in the facade I'd carefully constructed – that of the single mother who could handle anything. While I was accustomed to navigating life's difficulties as a single parent, this situation felt overwhelming and unfamiliar. I grappled with internal conflicts, including worries about El's path and, of course, my need for control and certainty, and dreaded failure as a parent.

These anxieties, coupled with societal pressures and my failure to manage this scenario effectively, often resulted in feelings of shame.

I masked my turmoil, presenting a facade of normalcy, but a mix of anger and confusion and a crippling lack of knowledge about how to navigate this situation crushed me. This absence of control, a stark contrast to my usual self-sufficiency, fuelled these feelings of fear, shame, and desperation.

My family had always been a source of strength, but in this moment, I didn't feel comfortable leaning on them. The thought of revealing my lack of control felt more terrifying than facing the situation alone, so I retreated, believing it was easier than seeking support. I then misinterpreted their silence as disapproval, deepening my sense of isolation. I felt rejected.

Extended family members also faced difficulties navigating these changes, leading to awkward interactions and decreased communication. Some friends and colleagues displayed inappropriate curiosity, treating El and our family as a spectacle or topic of gossip. Others used us as an opportunity to demonstrate their liberal open-mindedness. These behaviours caused discomfort and made me avoid further interactions.

Josie

As she witnessed El's challenging transition journey, a wave of negative emotions overwhelmed Josie, including worry, embarrassment, and difficulty processing the changes.

Josie withheld information from her friends as she struggled to process the situation. The family dynamic understandably shifted as my focus and support went towards El during this time, leaving Josie feeling isolated and disconnected.

At this time, Josie had had limited opportunities to understand transgender identities and the complexities of body dysphoria. Societal pressures and the limited visibility of transgender people also contributed to her challenges. She feared judgement from others, a common experience regardless of age – and Josie was only twenty.

Josie felt a lack of control over the situation and uncertainty about the future, which was deeply unsettling for her. I understood this reaction, as I was grappling with it myself.

A hesitant quietness often silenced Josie's vibrant and joyful spirit when she visited. Engaging in family conversations regarding El felt like navigating a minefield, and she would often stay quiet rather than risk saying the wrong thing or causing anxieties, further conflict, or hurt feelings.

However, Josie is today a fabulous big sister and supports El one hundred percent. As her understanding strengthened, she bolstered both El and me, even attempting to bridge the gap between other family members and encourage her father to become more supportive.

El's Father

I cannot speak extensively about El and Josie's father, David, and I have avoided making assumptions about his feelings based on limited information.

At first, David showed personal support for El. Nonetheless, manoeuvring through family dynamics turned out to be challenging, and I acknowledged that everyone adjusts to significant changes in their own way. David lived five hours from El, which brought about challenges in travel, communication, and understanding. Although David didn't confide in me about his worries, I'm certain he did with others.

Eventually, David subsidised El's last procedure, showcasing his commitment to her welfare in his own way. This action, ten years into El's transition, demonstrates his own personal evolution in his understanding and support, although his specific reasons remain personal and unexpressed to me.

Ten years ago, El wouldn't have dared ask her father for financial help with a procedure. His reaction to her transition had been indecisive, leaving her puzzled and uncomprehending. Her stepsister's wedding was an obvious instance of that.

Perhaps, as for me in the beginning, David's reaction stemmed from fear of the unknown, a societal pressure to conform, or simply insufficient understanding. His act of financial support, ten years later, was huge for El. It wasn't just about money; it was a silent apology, a testament to his personal evolution, and a bridge across the chasm of misunderstanding – a bridge that has since been fortified and cemented as their relationship goes from strength to strength.

Partner

My partner, Phil, held strong views regarding transgender individuals that were different from my own. While I understood that his initial discomfort stemmed from unfamiliarity with the topic, our contrasting perspectives on El's transition created challenges within the family.

Phil's initial response to El's transitioning reflected discomfort. Although Phil's discomfort wasn't rooted in religious beliefs, it was evident that societal pressures and anticipated reactions from others influenced this response to El's transitioning.

Phil felt extreme discomfort with El's gender nonconformity. Initially, I empathised with Phil's feelings to some extent; I, too, was still undergoing a learning process. However, my role as El's parent guided me to advocate for her health and happiness.

Phil's constant negativity towards El created a significant strain on our communication. To protect myself from the emotional toll of these interactions, I limited discussions about El with him. This decision, however, resulted in a growing sense of isolation within our relationship.

Phil's apprehension also stemmed from limited knowledge about body dysphoria and his misconceptions about El's future self-expression. Phil worried that El would exaggerate her femininity by dressing in a way he felt was overtly sexual – fishnet stockings and short skirts. El, however, always favoured comfortable clothing (jumper and leggings), and this preference would continue. Clothes for El have always been a necessity, not a fashion statement.

Trying to present a united front, Phil and I attended a session with El's therapist to get some insight and clarity in the situation we were facing. However, this visit only highlighted our contrasting viewpoints regarding El's transitioning. Phil expressed strong disagreement with the therapist's approach and believed she should discourage El's exploration of her gender identity. I disagreed with Phil and supported the therapist's inclusive, supportive stance regarding El's expressed needs. The chasm between us continued to grow.

I would like to take this opportunity to stress that it is crucial you find a therapist who prioritises your child's needs and provides appropriate support. El's therapist did not suggest to El that she might be transgender. El presented herself to the therapist as transgender and used their time to gain guidance on and knowledge of the subject.

As family relationships continued to be strained, Phil offered El the option to rent his house, which had become vacant, while she was transitioning.

I expressed reservations about this decision because of my concerns for El's welfare, but El's unwavering desire for independence led her to consider Phil's offer. I was all too familiar with El's remarkable ability to stick to her convictions once she decided, so ultimately, I respected her decision and allowed her to try living alone.

Although I hoped this would give us all the personal space we required at this time, in my heart, I felt it wasn't what El needed, and it worried me. With the constant struggles El encountered each day regarding getting treatment and support for her body dysphoria, she was already showing signs of deteriorating mental health.

After three months of living alone, El's living environment had deteriorated, and she needed additional support. El had spent these three months isolated in the house, neglecting basic housekeeping tasks and personal hygiene. By now, my concerns about her well-being were causing me anxiety and heightened distress, so I packed her bags and brought her back home.

Maintaining a positive relationship with Phil continued to prove challenging. While his anger about the state of his house was understandable, it eventually contributed to the breakdown of our relationship. I found myself alone again. Meanwhile, El's deteriorating mental state was also glaringly obvious.

Despite the difficulties, Phil and I today remain good friends. With time, our perspective, understanding of the situation, and communication have improved. We can now maintain a friendly relationship and even discuss El openly. Phil has acknowledged that his actions during that time stemmed from several factors. These included concerns about societal perceptions, potential strain on the relationship, and limited understanding based on his prior life and work experiences and influences.

Cousins

El's extended family members learned in 2014 that El was considering transitioning. El's cousins, Jimmy and Jane, expressed surprise.

Jane, a teacher with experience in supporting students who were exploring their gender, knew former pupils who had transitioned and now identified as a different gender from their assigned one at birth. In these cases, transitioning seemed to fit in with their personality and what she knew about them. It wasn't a surprise.

However, El's cousins expressed surprise upon learning about El's desire to transition. Their relationship with El had become distant over the years, and this may have been a factor in their reaction. In their younger years, the cousins had all been very close, but as they got older, their closeness dwindled. Feeling out of place, El now felt she had little in common with her cousins. El seemed quiet and withdrawn to them and had been for some time, and they were worried about her well-being.

Jimmy and Jane thought the wishes El expressed about transition might be associated with questions of belonging and identity. Our family has many strong, successful single females, and they felt that El might struggle to see where she fitted in with this close-knit band of women and that these feelings might be part of this.

It was not until Christmas 2017 that they saw Billy as El. They expressed admiration for El's bravery and a genuine desire to connect and offer support. However, they encountered challenges because of El's hesitance to engage in specific discussions and my own closed-off nature. They realised this was still a difficult subject to broach, so they avoided deeper discussion.

Discussing this topic with my family always proved difficult. My embarrassment, fear, and uncertainty made communication challenging for me. I struggled to express my anxieties about navigating the situation and hid my fear of being out of control and not coping well. Inadvertently, this made my family's well-intentioned attempts at support feel misdirected or insufficient, and my unspoken needs left them unsure of how to respond.

18

EXTERNAL ACCEPTANCE

As El continued with her transition and lived as a woman in public and private spaces, we occasionally attracted attention from others. While some individuals reacted with acceptance, others displayed negative or disapproving behaviours, such as rude comments and microaggressions. These situations were emotionally challenging for both El and me.

During one shopping trip, for instance, while El and I were browsing the clothing selection, a woman stopped and stared at us for a minute or two. The intensity of the stare felt intrusive, so I held her gaze until she moved away. We weren't causing any disruption; we were simply browsing clothes. We proceeded with our shopping trip, but the experience reminded us of the challenges we would face.

On a brighter note, we shared a positive experience while visiting Josie for her graduation from university. The trip was about shared experiences, strengthening the invisible threads that bound us together as a family. Josie, now the supportive sister, offered fashion advice while I revelled in El's new confidence. Conversations flowed freely, filled with laughter and a renewed sense of closeness. This wasn't just a shopping trip; it was a celebration of El's journey and the unwavering bond that held our family together.

Josie and I together experienced overwhelming jealousy over El's clothing size: six. The envy was real! How could El, with all the late-night snacking sessions, be a size six while Josie and I struggled? (We teased her, of course, all in good fun.)

Other recollections were less positive but provided glimpses of acceptance.

During this period, El was involved in a car accident, a sudden jolt amid her journey that cast a dark shadow. A new challenge presented itself – El had not legally changed her name on all documents.

At the scene of the accident, the process of sharing insurance information with the other driver, a regular obligation, evolved into an unexpected social experiment. Worry coiled within me as I explained the discrepancy between the name with which I referred to El and the name on her legal documents. But a simple nod of understanding from the driver calmed my anxieties. I received this brief interaction with appreciation, seeing it as a testament to basic human decency. I realised that acceptance existed beyond the limited circles in which I'd observed it.

For El, the adrenaline from the crash quickly diminished and was replaced by a dull ache in her neck. Wincing, she reached up to massage the sore spot. But amid the wreckage and discomfort, a warmth bloomed in her chest, and she smiled at me. The other driver, a woman with a kind voice, had addressed her correctly: '*Are you all right, miss?*'

It might not seem to qualify as a significant occasion, but for El, it represented a minor triumph. Being misgendered, constantly having to correct pronouns or explain her identity, was a daily occurrence. It undermined her confidence, making her feel unseen. For so long, she had fought for recognition, for the world to see her as she truly was – El, a woman. In that simple 'miss', El found a flicker of validation, a confirmation of her identity that washed over her like a soothing balm.

The ambulance took El to our local hospital, and I followed. However, the straightforward task of checking in at the hospital reception morphed into frustration for El. As the receptionist addressed her by her legal name, Billy, a grimace contorted El's face. Each interaction, each pronoun that didn't resonate with her identity, chipped away at her sense of self. As I witnessed her silent struggle, a wave of anger engulfed me. The staff's repeated mistake regarding El's name, although unintentional, contributed to El's emotional distress, which I believe should have been avoided.

Thankfully, El escaped major injuries. After a few hours, they discharged El, and I brought her home.

Throughout the next three years, we battled with ongoing issues: getting blood tests and appointments, navigating workplace bathrooms and clothing choices, and confusion from family and friends, including challenges with Christmas gift buying. Somehow, the act of purchasing gifts for Christmas filled me with apprehension. Occasionally I bought El hair straighteners, perfume, and make-up, but mostly I played it safe. When buying clothes, I focused on neutral options, hoping El would like them and that they wouldn't cause any discomfort within the family. Finding a middle ground was an undertaking – discovering pyjamas that had a feminine touch while also being perceived as gender neutral. Other clothes I chose followed the same logic. I found T-shirts with little flowers that weren't flamboyant or outlandish. They all maintained a subtle presence, but I was giving it my all. Meanwhile, my family didn't know where to start!

El's emotional state fluctuated, but it became increasingly clear that her mental well-being was deteriorating as the years went by and her goals remained elusive.

We moved to a secluded area, a small hamlet surrounded by fields, seeking a peaceful environment for El to explore her identity freely. El would spend a lot of time walking Molly, our beautiful Westie, and feeding the local horses in nearby stables.

I hoped the move would offer El a fresh start, a chance to improve her mental health and feel safe in a new environment where we could continue our journey privately.

19

MENTAL HEALTH

El's mental health had steadily declined over the years and continued to do so, despite my best efforts and the fresh start of a new house. The exhaustion and frustration of transitioning took its toll on her. The scheduled blood tests at the GP, along with the societal obstacles El encountered, only heightened her stress and anxiety. She could achieve her desired appearance only if she had substantial amounts of money.

El dealt with complex personal challenges around her physical characteristics and how those interacted with her developing sense of self. Because she'd experienced male puberty, certain physical features caused her great discomfort. Her desire to address these aspects of her appearance, such as facial hair and facial features, stemmed from a desire to better align her physical self with her desired gender identity.

El was also uneasy about her own voice, though it wasn't deep. Although transgender men can receive hormones to deepen their voices, the hormones El received didn't help her achieve a more womanly voice. Instead, this issue can be addressed through either voice therapy and training or a surgical procedure on the vocal cords.

El experienced physical pain when observing her physical characteristics in the mirror. Seeing her reflection caused her heart to ache. She was clear about the treatments she desired. The NHS did not cover these treatments, also referred to as facial feminisation surgery (FFS).

FFS is a series of plastic surgery procedures designed to create a more feminine facial appearance for transgender women undergoing gender affirmation treatment. The operations aim to reduce prominent masculine features and achieve a naturally feminine look.

The procedures involved in FFS are based on individual needs and priorities. These procedures can reshape the forehead, brows, nose, cheeks, and jaw, as well as minimise the appearance of an Adam's apple (performed through a tracheal shave). Besides plastic surgery, facial feminisation procedures may include non-surgical treatments, such as injections for wrinkle reduction and facial sculpting (using fillers and Botox).

In the UK, the NHS does not cover FFS for transitioning adults. The average cost for receiving FFS privately ranges from £30,000 (in Thailand or Spain) to £50,000 (in the USA).

As time went on with no options for FFS available within the NHS, El showed noticeable behavioural and physical changes, and her mental health declined. Her symptoms included social isolation, neglect of hygiene, and intense mood swings characterised by rage and, I would soon learn, self-inflicted harm. She no longer laughed, smiled, or even spoke as before.

Overwhelmed by the disparity between the woman she was and the reflection she saw in the mirror, El longed for FFS. Between the prohibitive cost and the lack of NHS options, it seemed we'd reached a dead end. Bridging the gap seemed hopeless, and both of us plunged into despair. She felt like she didn't matter, that society didn't value her enough to offer her timely treatment. This fed into her sense of hopelessness and helplessness about her future.

I felt helpless too. I could see the pain this was causing El, and I desperately tried but failed to find a solution. Despite all my research, I found no way to get support for FFS in the UK, and the cost to complete it was astronomical. We now found ourselves in a desolate state because we didn't have a clear path to follow.

El had fabulous long, thick hair, full of natural curls. We were all envious of her. But as El's struggles continued and her interest in self-care declined, it became tangled and matted, an external symbol reflecting her inner despair. Faced with El's neglected, damaged hair, together we made the heartbreaking decision to cut it short. As I took each snip, tears streamed down my face, exposing the depth of my sorrow. It was impossible to bear the realisation that we'd reached such a low point. I believed I had let El down by not shielding her from her suffering, but I didn't know how to rescue her.

Afterward, I held El close in my arms until morning, the weight of desolation a suffocating presence. Even today, this memory evokes a wave of tears. Fear and impotence overwhelmed me as I thought about El's mental state. This marked a rock bottom for the two of us.

Rock bottom number two was the horrifying discovery of El clutching a knife in her room. The vulnerability etched on her face was a stark contrast to the determination of the young woman I knew, and it paralysed me. Any illusion of control I'd clung to shattered. What had brought her to this point? Was the weight of the transition becoming unbearable? Or did deeper emotional struggles lie hidden beneath the surface?

The dread that had been simmering within me intensified, a cold anxiety that threatened to devour me. In that moment, torn between wanting to help and fearing I'd make things worse, I felt helpless, alone, and very, very frightened. I now knew El was self-harming, and it broke me. I contacted my sister, a mental health professional, desperate for help.

We pleaded with El to go for counselling, but El resisted, retreating behind a wall of silence. I spent many nights sleeping in her room to keep her safe. It was a period filled with indescribable worry and a desperate longing to support her in every way possible.

El's mental health struggles continued, and despite my support, I also grappled with a range of difficult emotions of my own. Fear, frustration, and even resentment arose within me. Why couldn't I make her suffering disappear? I felt an intense mix of anger and frustration because of my powerlessness. A portion of me held resentment towards her attempts to cope with her pain.

While these emotions may sound insensitive, they came from a place of profound love and a desperation to see El well. They stemmed from my inability to ease her pain. El's self-harm exposed a raw nerve – the shame fuelled by societal stigmas I never knew I harboured. Should I keep this a secret, adding to the burden of all the secrets I was carrying and the embarrassment caused by this secrecy? Was discussing it an admission of failure? I remember this as a time of immense vulnerability and isolation affecting us both, with no apparent solutions in sight.

Days blurred into nights. Worry was a constant companion. The challenges El faced mirrored the storm within me – fear, frustration, a relentless barrage of anxieties. Exhaustion gnawed at me, fuelled by my growing fear for her mental well-being.

While I supported El, I couldn't deny the conflicting emotions swirling within me. A piece of me clung to the gem of information gleaned at the beginning of my research, which held that 80 percent of those who identified as transgender would desist from transitioning. I didn't know if there was any truth in it, but it was a glimmer of hope that things could go back to the way they used to be. Desperate and exhausted, I craved an end to the emotional turmoil and a return to a familiar routine for us both.

Sometimes I hoped that El's despair would make her change her mind. I knew this was wrong and unkind. In my frantic state, I resorted to a coping mechanism that, in hindsight, wasn't ideal. I compartmentalised my emotions and anxieties, tucking them away in a mental box and refusing to acknowledge or explore them. This approach allowed me to continue to function day-to-day, but it also prevented me from fully understanding and processing my experience and feelings.

Fear and worry were my constant nemesis. Forty percent of respondents to 2015's US Transgender Survey, carried out by the National Center for Transgender Equality, said they had attempted suicide. I knew El was in a dark place and feared she thought about suicide often. El's challenges caused great worry for everyone in the family. We all saw her pain, and the terror of losing her weighed heavily on us. Panic gripped me as I contemplated the possibility of tragedy.

I tried to watch El more closely. I observed the changes in her behaviour, including withdrawal and social isolation. I felt an overwhelming urge to protect her, but fear also held me back. I was worried that she was making the wrong choice, and I could not gather the courage to ask questions; I dreaded the answers. I hesitated to talk frankly with her about her struggles. In hindsight, many of my decisions in those days were based on fear.

El's withdrawal from social interaction also drew uninformed criticism from some who mistook it for laziness. Others suggested I was indulging her behaviour. These comments were hurtful and unhelpful. I distanced myself from such negativity, choosing instead to focus on creating a safe and supportive environment for El.

Although my family didn't understand El's journey, they avoided outright opposition. They didn't outwardly object: El was an adult, after all. However, their unease with the situation was clear. This created an uncomfortable tension, which only added to the stress we were all experiencing. My mother, especially, expressed concern about my health. Drained and always anxious for El, I found myself in a state of confusion. How could I ease the anguish for everyone involved?

For El, time now seemed to stand still. She had no job and did little more than lie in her room in her pyjamas, watching TV and playing on the internet with the companionship of our dog, Molly. All I could do was provide a safe place and ensure she was eating. I was scared that El would withdraw from the world altogether. I felt she had given up. As her mother, it was unbearable to witness.

THE U-TURN

After four years filled with relentless hurdles and emotional strain in her pursuit of medical transition, El made the heartbreaking decision to detransition, confiding in me she didn't experience the boost in confidence she had expected upon identifying as a woman. Ultimately, she felt she could not fully express her gender identity without FFS.

I am ashamed to say that I didn't take the time to delve further into her explanation or understand the immense pain behind it. Instead, I danced around the room, elated that my son was back and that we could now put all of this behind us. I told El her decision was welcome but that I would support her should she change her mind, though a part of me secretly hoped this would never happen. Instead of delving deeper, my initial focus was on my sense of relief.

Initially, I'd taken pride in supporting El's journey of self-discovery, believing that providing her space to explore her gender identity had resulted in a positive outcome. However, upon reflection, I recognise that my support may not have been as comprehensive or unconditional as I believed.

While my intentions were positive, the limitations of my approach and my secret hope that El would change her mind might have contributed to her struggles, until it all became too difficult and she did a U-turn.

I now understand the reasons for El's U-turn, and I'm filled with shame for disregarding her suffering while focusing on my own welfare.

As El has expressed, her reason for the U-turn was her constant suicidal thoughts and self-harm. She knew these were causing me immense pain, stress, and worry. She also believed that without FFS, she would not make a sufficiently convincing woman. She saw no way forward, just a half-life. The climb seemed insurmountable.

One of her close friends had also recently tried to commit suicide, and witnessing the pain friends and family endured because of this, as well as her having to deal with her own emotions about it, made her decide to try to live as a man again.

She wanted to cut off the thing that was causing these thoughts, which was primarily the body dysphoria. She tried to believe that if she no longer sought to transition, she would eliminate her worry about her appearance, and then the suicidal thoughts would go too. Her decision was never based on confusion about what she wanted; it was motivated by the pain and upset she saw the process was causing for people she loved and cared about.

She therefore suppressed her own happiness, prioritising the well-being of those she cared for.

21

THE WILDERNESS YEARS

Soon after this conversation, Billy, as El now was once more, visited a friend and returned with a changed appearance. He had decided to discontinue hormone therapy, and he'd cut his hair short and grown a beard. A wide smile spread across my face. I was unable to contain my happiness. We would be back to normal, whatever normal meant.

Billy hoped seeing his best mate at uni and getting involved in the atmosphere would help him integrate back into the male world. He explored different ways of living and expressing himself, seeking support from his friend and aiming for a sense of belonging.

The experience gave him some confidence that he could live as a man. But this was short-lived. On one journey back from visiting his best friend, a weathered sign, barely visible beneath clinging vines, caught Billy's eye. *Dead End*, it proclaimed in stark lettering. The realisation hit him like a physical blow. He was heading down the wrong path. Without hesitation, he slammed on the brakes, the screech of tyres announcing his abrupt course correction.

It was as if the change in direction had jolted his brain, clearing away the fog that had obscured his vision. He wasn't sure where the new path would lead, but in the clarity that washed over him, he found a beacon in the darkness. He gripped the steering wheel, a determined glint in his eyes, ready to face whatever lay ahead on his chosen journey. Billy knew now that his feelings would not change, but he also knew that if he started the transition process again, he would be in the same desperate situation.

Recognising the challenges he'd previously faced, Billy focused on his mental health and financial well-being so that he would be better prepared next time. At this point he did not mention his intentions to me. He just went into planning mode. And I went into 'making my son's life as good as possible' mode.

22

LIFE AS BILLY

I threw myself into improving my son's self-esteem and future. We looked at career options, starting with his loves and likes in life.

Billy had struggled with attending an external college in the past, so we researched online courses within his chosen area of study, animal care. He successfully completed his chosen online course and received the qualification he required. As luck would have it, a vacancy soon turned up at a local animal day care centre. Billy's hard work paid off as he secured the job and wasted no time in getting started.

After six months, we looked into the possibility of obtaining a mortgage. He possessed a substantial deposit from family money and now enjoyed a secure regular wage. Despite his financial constraints, we found a small terraced house in a cul-de-sac that needed extensive updating.

The small, charming terraced house, bathed in warm sunlight, exuded an aura of possibility. The period features whispered of history, the sunny courtyard promised a haven for relaxation, and the convenient location ticked all the right boxes. It warmed my heart to witness the spark of excitement in Billy's eyes as he envisioned his future in this house. This wasn't just a purchase; it was a stepping stone on his journey towards a life I hoped he could call his own.

I harboured a fervent hope – that the house, a symbol of accomplishment, would rekindle Billy's sense of achievement. I longed for Billy's mental health to flourish, his self-esteem to soar. I longed to show Billy the improvements that life could offer now that he'd embraced living life as a male.

I knew Billy needed his own space to spread his wings and thrive. But amid this realisation, a truth dawned – I, too, craved space. The toll of witnessing my son's daily struggles had been heavy. The stress of watching your child in pain is indescribable, and I wanted to be there for him, but not all day, every day! This realisation led me to seek some long-needed self-care.

I convinced myself that this house was for Billy, but it was also for me. It provided a temporary balm, masking the guilt and inadequacy I felt for not fully supporting Billy's transition. Yes, I helped buy it, driven by the need for more space, love for Billy, and a desire to ease my guilt and show Billy that he had a brighter future as a male. The weighty paperwork was a stark contrast to the lightness of hope in my heart.

Now that Billy was living as a man again, the paralysing fear I had been experiencing for his future fell away, and I threw myself into helping modernise his house and create a secure, warm space he could call home and be proud of. His best friend moved in as a lodger to help with the mortgage and bills. Billy's new independence brought tranquillity, allowing both of us the space to explore new possibilities. Life for me, once shrouded in uncertainty, now shimmered with possibility. It was filled with positivity and hope as El detransitioned to Billy and I started a new relationship.

Telling close relations about El's U-turn led to told-you-so comments reiterating that El's transition had been a phase or a form of attention-seeking. These barely troubled me, as the paralysing fear I had carried for my child's future had vanished overnight. I'd regained the ability to breathe again.

It was eye-opening to realise how much tension and stress I had been carrying. As the weight lifted, a wave of relief washed over me. The release was pure liberation. The physical and emotional tolls had both been immense, not to mention the financial burden.

PART TWO:

MY JOURNEY

MY BACKGROUND

To grasp my personal journey of acceptance alongside El's, it's necessary to understand the person I used to be and who I am now. They are two different people, and this transition came about because of El's journey, my fear for her future, my pain during this time, and my personal inner traumas. They all collided in one powerful moment that led to a re-evaluation of myself: Who was I truly? And who did I aspire to become?

Let me tell you a little about myself.

I was born in October 1963, in Sturry, Canterbury, a beautiful town in Kent, but my mother and older sister and I spent most of my early years on a council estate in the Midlands. My father was an alcoholic and was physically abusive to my mother. Before I was born, he had already departed in favour of one of his many lady friends.

Despite premature birth, health complications, and the absence of a father, I arrived with a fighting spirit, overcoming these initial obstacles. Yellow with jaundice, big brown eyes, and a quiff of black hair – that's how my mother remembers me.

It quickly became apparent to my mother that despite the challenges of my entrance into this world, I was ready to confront it.

We moved for 'many a new start' during my father's various sporadic visits – I believe we counted seventeen moves in all – before we finally settled in the Midlands without him.

I was eight then, and my sister was nine. We completed our last move overnight. For me, this sudden move entailed attending school one day, telling my friends that we were moving, leaving that evening, and starting a new school the next.

Memories of my father from my childhood and teenage years are scarce, limited to interactions I initiated as I sought connection in my teenage years. Unfortunately, repeated rejections and disappointments led to a complete disconnect from my father, and we have not had contact since.

My memory of our family's sudden move remains vivid. I was young and didn't grasp the full situation, only that things were different and Dad wasn't with us anymore.

It was undeniably an exciting time. I can still picture myself clad in my favourite white tights and skirt, clackers flying between my eager hands as I played with my friends in the crowded playground. Announcing our impending move to be closer to our cousins was akin to boasting of a winning lottery ticket. Thankfully, the grown-up considerations and financial worries that rippled through our lives were invisible to my young mind.

Once we moved, my excitement dwindled significantly as we found ourselves living in a cramped maisonette where I shared a bedroom and a bunk with my older sister. This transition brought various challenges for our family. Getting accustomed to a new environment, dealing with a limited income, and supporting ourselves were collaborative endeavours. Thankfully, we received help from the council, allowing us to have meals at school and helping us settle in.

For everyone else, summer meant freedom: rather than eating a hot meal in the canteen, they brought packed lunches so they could sit on the playing fields. It wasn't so for me. Unlike my friends, who unpacked colourful feasts from brown paper bags, I had to go to the hot lunches, or free school dinners, every day. I would run into the canteen, eat my food as quickly as I could, and then dash to the school playing field, where my friends were eating their chosen packed lunches. I resented this exclusion. It appeared to be a small detail, but it had a distinct effect on me, causing me to experience a feeling of being left out of their world. Yet no matter how much I implored my mother for sandwiches, she refused to give in.

Middle school was a hyper-focused social battlefield, and uniforms were a key part of the game. Unlike the store-bought versions sported by most classmates, my uniform and my sister's bore the unmistakable stamp of being homemade. The moment I stepped into the middle school hallway in my homemade uniform, I felt a spotlight I wished to escape. The others' crisp, identical uniforms seemed to mock mine, with its slightly uneven stitching and fabric. Fitting in had become an all-consuming goal for me, and this uniform, a symbol of difference, felt like a giant red flag waving the opposite message.

Holiday

As a young child, I would often take myself away to a world of make-believe. I'd spend hours lost in the world at the bottom of my nan's garden, the field and the spinney beyond that, seeking solace and creativity in an expanse of wildflowers and butterflies. The garden was a portal to another world. Fields of wildflowers stretched beyond, a kaleidoscope of colours swaying in the breeze. Monarch butterflies, their wings like stained glass, flitted among the fragrant flowers.

I spent many afternoons gathering sweet-smelling petals from my nan's treasured roses, which I then used to create my own concoction. With a little help from the sun and a few salvaged pots and pans, I'd transform them into a fragrant rose water.

The air would fill with the sweet aroma of the petals as they steeped, and the final product, a delicate pink water, captured the very essence of those lazy afternoons. Even a slight whiff of roses today transports me back to those lazy summer afternoons, a time of endless possibilities and a heart brimming with childish wonder.

Sturry became a summer playground for my cousin, my sister, and me. Our days were a whirlwind of make-believe adventures. Regardless of whether we were constructing elaborate forts out of furniture or attending to our imaginary patients with unwavering dedication, Nan consistently served as a silent supporter in the background.

The highlight of each summer was the open-air bus ride to Margate. With pockets full of saved-up coins, we'd pile onto the sunshine-drenched bus, a sense of adventure thrumming through us. Dreamland awaited: a wonderland of carousels, candy floss, and heart-stopping rides. Ice cream dripped down our chins, laughter bubbled over, and the day stretched out before us, a delicious blend of freedom and sugary treats. Catching the last bus back was a constant worry as we pushed the limits of playtime, but the sight of Nan waiting at the gate, her face a mixture of concern and relief, was a familiar comfort.

The allure of the seaside proved impossible to resist. Many a cool summer morning began with promises of good behaviour and packed lunches, only to end with us ditching our costumes in favour of a refreshing dip in the waves. Soaked to the bone and grinning from ear to ear, we'd return home, sandcastle remnants clinging to our skin and the salty tang of the ocean in our hair. While Nan might have grumbled playfully about our disregard for dry clothes, those carefree days spent building sandcastles and chasing seagulls are some of my most treasured memories of childhood.

I also remember Christmases camping in the front room with my cousins on inflatable mattresses and hiding behind the settee with hands over my ears as Grandad expertly managed to extricate the balloon from going up the open fire chimney.

Grandad wasn't your typical Santa. He drove a three-wheeler turquoise car, a testament to some past workplace mishap, that sported a gaping hole in the side. Yet for us, it was the coolest vehicle on the road. Each morning, we'd race to the front room window, eager to wave him off to work and glimpse that infamous hole.

Education

At school, I was an average student but loved and excelled at all sports. I represented my school in swimming, cross country, gymnastics, and athletics. I loved the summer terms, when I spent most of my time playing in all the inter-team sports activities and revelled in my popularity, being chosen for all sporting events. Like all children, I was keen to be popular and well-liked, but for me that need was an especially powerful one, as an absent father made me fear rejection of any kind. I craved positive social connections and actively sought to be liked and accepted by my peers. I had already cultivated the role of people pleaser.

My family structure, unlike those of my friends, was unconventional, and I felt isolated by that difference. The urgency to close this social gap spurred me to work harder, leading to consistent application across all subjects. The smell of books and the feel of pen on paper became constants in my days. I worked hard at school and tried to be proficient in all areas.

Witnessing my mother's strength and determination instilled a strong work ethic in me. However, her struggles also highlighted the limitations imposed by our background. College seemed like a distant dream, and career options appeared restricted by our financial circumstances. My social circle didn't offer many examples of professional success, and the world beyond our immediate struggles felt vast and unknown. This instilled a deep desire to break free from these perceived limitations and forge my path to security and fulfilment. I believed that happiness in life was achieved only through external validation, material gain, and professional success.

As I progressed on my journey, determined to reach these goals, I adopted a flexible approach, responding to opportunities as they arose through intuition and initiative. As I met and overcame life's challenges, I often received what I needed, sometimes unexpectedly, and this always led me down a path I hadn't foreseen, but which ultimately was a better one.

I developed a passion for sports at school and outside, which fuelled my desire to become a PE teacher. However, this path was obstructed, as no one expected me to gain the qualifications to fulfil my dream.

Not knowing what to do, my mother said, 'Learn to type!' I took her advice and enrolled in a college course that also incorporated business studies. I immediately went from an average student at school to an A student at college. I had found my niche. I worked hard over the next two years and completed the course.

When I was eighteen, with an engagement ring on my finger and a future seemingly set, a different path started calling to me. The desire to build a fulfilling career and explore my professional potential burned brighter than the prospect of settling down right away. The decision to break my engagement was difficult, but I knew I needed to prioritise my own aspirations.

I went into full-time work as a marketing assistant in a local cosmetics company. It was a good job, but while I was there, my constant craving to achieve more inspired me to go back to education. University was not a topic of discussion in our household while I was growing up. It just wasn't an option. We always assumed in our household that my sister and I would go into employment from school. We didn't even consider any other options.

My sister was a nurse all her working life. She never wanted to be anything else. She found her purpose and passion at an early age. I spent many play days as a pretend patient wrapped in bandages, being made better by my sister, the nurse.

In retrospect, I understand that my younger self had internalised the belief that university was only for those who excelled academically. Yet my yearning for personal and professional growth burned far brighter than those doubts. Fuelled by this desire, I challenged the limiting messages I'd internalised and gave university a shot.

I began a two-year night school Higher National Certificate in business studies, aiming for a distinction that would be equivalent to a university degree and grant me entry into Liverpool Polytechnic's postgraduate marketing management programme. I poured my heart into those two years and achieved the coveted distinction.

Liverpool greeted me with open arms, but my bank account told a different story. Rent loomed large, and with limited funds and no possibility of help from family, the dream of university seemed to slip away. Dejected, I started packing my bags to return home.

My kind and perceptive landlord, upon sensing my despair, intervened with a lifeline. 'Can you cook?' he asked. My heart leaped. It wasn't the most glamorous solution, but it was a chance. I readily agreed, and so began my adventure as a student-chef, whipping up meals for my housemates in exchange for a roof over my head. I'll never forget that landlord's generosity; it allowed me to stay the course and pursue my goals. I also met my husband Bobby while studying in Liverpool.

Career Path

Fuelled by my success, I landed several executive positions culminating in a coveted position as marketing director at a drinks company by the age of twenty-nine. However, the corporate world, while challenging, wasn't offering the same level of fulfilment I craved. Then the late-eighties recession hit, and the company folded. This unexpected event, coupled with the end of my marriage to Bobby, forced me to re-evaluate my path.

I chose not to pursue employment again. Instead, on an impulse, I went with my intuition and started a business. Entrepreneurship had always held a certain mystique for me.

The concept of starting a project from the beginning, making decisions, and having control over my work was appealing. While my desire for external validation still lingered, it was now intertwined with a yearning for autonomy and the satisfaction of creating something of my own.

Finding myself alone and unemployed, I discovered a government programme called the Enterprise Allowance Scheme. It provided rent and unemployment benefits while I started a business, and I found a small cottage to rent. Incredibly, that business is still thriving thirty-two years later.

There have been many occasions when my company nearly folded because of personal situations or external influences. Each time, I found someone who extended a lifeline, and I seized the opportunity to survive. In 1993, I met the father of my children and moved to Cornwall with my business three years later. Josie was born in 1994 and Billy in 1996. Our relationship ended in 2001, leading to our separation, and I returned to the Midlands.

The banking crisis of 2008 affected my business, nearly causing us to lose our house and my hard-earned financial security. I had to act swiftly to reduce overhead costs. Fortunately, a lifeline emerged from a company I'd collaborated with on and off for years. They were also facing struggles, so we joined forces. I brought long-term customers, marketing, and sales expertise to the table, while they offered manufacturing and technical support. It was a perfect synergy.

The decision to close my factory and make staff redundant was difficult, but the merger with my new business partner proved successful. Within twelve months, we were both back in profit, and our partnership remains strong today. It also allowed me to be a full-time mum to my two children, taking them to school and picking them up, as well as being present during vacations.

Later, as market conditions worsened, I supplemented my income by assisting students at a local college. This role provided a welcome change of pace, getting me out of the house, allowing me to interact with people, and offering some extra income. I thrived in this role for four years.

While acting as a learning support worker at the college, I developed an interest in teaching. This experience brought me to the realisation that I could pursue a career in education. My constant drive for self-improvement and external validation once again pushed me towards personal growth.

Teaching hadn't crossed my mind since leaving school. However, possessing a degree and extensive business experience, I pursued a qualification to become a business studies teacher. I embraced the opportunity to achieve a childhood dream that had been previously denied.

Fresh off the breakup with Phil in the depths of winter 2018, the long, dark nights felt isolating. To manage my anxieties about Billy and fill the empty hours, I opted to return to studying.

I successfully obtained my Qualified Teacher Learning and Skills status as a business studies teacher in May 2018. However, I wasn't sure how I would utilise this qualification. My only teaching experience involved assisting students in a classroom setting. The thought of leading the class from the front filled me with fear. It was a daunting prospect.

Covid cut my exploration of teaching short. Schools closed, and my business suffered another blow. As a limited company, I wasn't eligible for government help. I needed to find an additional income source quickly, though I hoped my business would recover.

When schools reopened, I took a leap of faith and entered the teaching world. Today, I still teach. What began as a personal quest for learning and growth became my financial lifeline after Covid. Once again, I had found a way to survive and support my children.

Looking back, I recognise I have spent much of my life in survival mode because of external and internal circumstances. It's challenging to envision alternative paths when immediate needs constantly consume your time. Financial security and stability for me and my children became overwhelming concerns, leaving little room to consider other options.

The relentless pursuit of financial stability, control, external validation, and constant growth pushed me to take risks and embrace continuous learning. However, it also caused me to neglect deeper desires – the need for belonging, for a sense of fitting in, and to feel enough.

I was no stranger to vulnerability, but I never allowed such feelings to surface, denying them time or relevance. Instead, I chased external success and validation, hoping to diminish them. Failure wasn't an option; neither was compassion nor forgiveness for any missteps. My inner critic was relentless.

Attaining a single goal merely propelled me toward pursuing the next one. The need for external validation was a bottomless pit, its satisfaction fleeting. Each new achievement, I convinced myself, would bring ultimate happiness – but that remained elusive. A nagging sense of inadequacy shadowed me, and this was a secret I fiercely guarded.

Though I'd achieved financial independence and some career success, my personal life lacked the same upward trajectory.

My intense desire to be liked often led to people-pleasing, even at the expense of my own preferences. Saying no felt like a betrayal, and keeping promises, regardless of the cost to myself, took priority. My fear of rejection was so deeply ingrained that even minor criticism could cripple me with anxiety.

I craved certainty in all aspects of life. This aversion to anything unpredictable fuelled my anxieties around failure and rejection. The depth of my emotions often overwhelmed me, a root of shame that I desperately avoided. Limiting beliefs suffocated my inner needs. My mantra: Be successful, achieve, acquire material trophies, and happiness will follow.

My relationship history mirrored this internal turmoil. I cycled through relationships, lacking commitment and a true understanding of my own emotions. Some ended, while others dragged on long past their expiration date. The common thread, the reason for their demise? Me.

Fear of neediness and rejection crippled my ability to connect. Self-reliance, a strength I cultivated, also became a barrier to intimacy. I grappled with inadequacy, struggling to feel worthy of love. How could I give love when I couldn't love myself?

The independence I'd craved since childhood felt like the only path to happiness – a dangerous illusion. Ironically, I was drawn to those who needed me, a dynamic that inflated my sense of worth only to trigger my dread of abandonment and push them away. The relentless cycle continued, its grip unnoticed by me.

24

LIFE'S CURVEBALLS

ollowing Covid's devastating impact on my business, the next few years were a fight for survival. I juggled teaching four days a week to bolster my finances with stabilising the business.

Meanwhile, life continued for Billy and me. I felt immense relief and happiness that his detransition seemed successful. Nothing could be as difficult as those earlier years, not even new financial challenges. 'I can handle anything,' I often told myself, 'just not that again.'

Imagine my shock and utter despair when, in 2021, Billy visited and confessed that despite his valiant effort to live as a man, he needed to live authentically as a woman and complete his transition. As restrictions lifted and life returned to normal, El – as Billy now was once more – announced her intention to undergo facial feminisation surgery (FFS), the one procedure that had eluded her before.

The house I'd renovated with love and financial investment offered a surprising twist. Selling it could provide the funds for El's surgery. My actions, some selfish (I'd wanted Billy to live separately from me), had unintentionally provided the means for him to complete his journey. Soaring house prices meant a sale could allow him to finish what he started years ago.

I felt a surge of hurt and betrayal. The conversation that followed was fraught. We explored alternative financing, like a home equity loan, but though El promised to investigate all avenues, she insisted that selling the house remain an option.

Seeing my distress caused El pain, but her resolve was unwavering. She was an adult, and despite my resurfacing fears, I knew I had to support her. So I took a deep breath, and for a second time we embarked on a journey. Hormone therapy resumed, targeting facial hair reduction, breast development, and a more feminine figure.

Sharing El's decision with my family once more proved to be extremely challenging, even more so on this second occasion. El and I became a close-knit unit, shielding ourselves from outside discussions on the matter. My stomach once again involuntary clenched, and the unwelcome sickening sensation settled itself in the pit of my stomach.

Unfortunately, my personal relationship crumbled under the weight of these challenges. My dread of rejection resurfaced, and I retreated to protect myself. This wasn't ideal, considering my Covid-affected business struggled to stay afloat. We had also lost our beloved Westie, Molly.

Once again, despite my best efforts, I watched my business decline and my hard-fought financial security vanish.

25

A YEAR OF CHALLENGES

During the same year, 2021, I experienced a personal betrayal that left me feeling isolated and alone. People I had supported and considered friends decided I no longer fitted in. Their cruelty lacked justification, but it triggered my childhood trauma around rejection, leaving me deeply wounded.

The emotional pain from the betrayal, my crumbling relationship, a failing business, losing Molly, and El's re-transitioning sent me spiralling into an emotional abyss. I had a strong sense of being out of control, with no assurance left in my world. I imploded. It was my breaking point, and I crumbled.

El's house, which I'd poured myself into emotionally and financially, was meant to be a source of happiness for her. Over time, I'd become conditioned by materialism, believing possessions held the secret to happiness. This fuelled my resistance to selling the house – I clung fiercely to the dream of El owning a home.

This series of personal challenges greatly affected my mental well-being. They triggered a resurgence of inner anxieties, leading to emotional distress, anxiety, and depression. The personal betrayal I faced was one of the most hurtful experiences of my life. The resulting pain was incapacitating and agonising, leaving me feeling completely devastated. It was the worst kind of rejection, shattering my sense of security and leaving me emotionally vulnerable. I felt cracked open by the suffering.

My fear for El's future affected my daily life. I now struggled to perform even basic tasks and participate in professional and social activities. My lack of control fuelled my fear, shrouding me in a darkness that I struggled to navigate.

The strong, independent persona I'd meticulously cultivated over the years crumbled. In its place, a raw current of anxiety and fear pulsed through me. Functioning, working, or even being around people became impossible.

The ground beneath my feet had vanished, leaving me adrift in a sea of uncertainty. The fight seemed to have left me this time. I felt utterly lost, with no map or compass to guide me. Questions swirled in my mind: *How did this happen? What else is coming?* The urge to curl into a ball, to retreat from the world and its pain, was overwhelming. Why was any of this happening to *me*? It felt undeserved, and I did not know how to survive it.

For so long, I'd relentlessly pursued financial and personal achievement, convinced they were the key to happiness. Despite my surface appearance of success, I now felt like I was treading water, constantly on the edge of drowning.

I had to acknowledge my emotional inner turmoil and recognise my need for support. With the unwavering support of my two children, I reached out to my GP and close friends. Their compassion guided me onto a path towards recovery, which initially included medication and therapy.

I considered myself lucky to have El, someone who truly comprehended vulnerability, depression, and anxiety. With her gentle support and that of my daughter Josie, I began to heal.

26

A JOURNEY OF SELF-DISCOVERY

The first few weeks of counselling were difficult. I remember tearfully pouring out my emotions, and I'll never forget the therapist's compassionate and kind treatment. It was a powerful reminder that even a stranger's empathy can rekindle feelings of worth and hope. That moment stands out as a beacon in my journey.

This safe environment provided the opportunity to surrender and truly understand my traumas and limiting beliefs. I remember saying, 'I'm all in, one hundred percent. No resistance. I embrace this journey.' I began to grasp my role in my life's events. From this place of pain, I set out on a personal odyssey back to health.

My understanding deepened with each step. I explored my personal beliefs and their limitations, unearthed inner traumas, confronted fears, and challenged ego-driven thoughts. This journey led to a profound understanding of myself and my connection to my own well-being. I grieved for losing my friends and began to forge an alternative path and connections.

Understanding that I did not have the power to manage everything or anything, I made a deliberate decision. I stopped, stepped back from what troubled me, and committed to releasing control and resistance. In its place, I found clarity.

My therapist suggested exploring my 'inner child wounds', an idea that surprised me. Despite my father leaving our family early on, I'd never considered my upbringing unstable, thanks to my mother's love.

Comparing myself to others who'd lost a parent through more dramatic circumstances, I questioned whether my anxieties and feelings of unworthiness were overreactions. However, as therapy progressed, I recognised the obvious presence of an abandonment wound and its impact on my adult life.

The techniques my therapist used were unconventional. I drew pictures of myself as a child, answered questions using crayons in my left hand, and even spoke to myself as an adult would to a small child. While these practices might seem unusual, they were surprisingly effective in helping me connect with my inner child's buried emotions and needs. Recognising and understanding these needs, long suffocated by limiting beliefs, was a revelation.

Fear of abandonment loomed large, driving me to adopt the people-pleasing persona. Vulnerability? A foreign concept. I recall how, even as a young child, I mentioned my parents' divorce to friends almost as a throwaway comment, as if it held no weight for me. Detachment and emotional disengagement became my coping mechanisms at a very early age. It was too terrifying to feel. I remember thinking about my father and muttering defiantly, 'Watch this space. I'm going to be successful.'

This fear of abandonment had permeated my life. Throughout childhood and adulthood, I experienced a sense of being on the outside, even among those closest to me. My adult relationships followed a similar pattern. I clung to unhealthy ones far too long and gravitated towards emotionally unavailable partners. Ironically, if someone showed genuine emotional availability, I abruptly ended things, fearing hurt. Only now was I seeing the repetitive pattern in my actions.

THE PURSUIT OF HAPPINESS – A MISGUIDED PATH

L osing financial security was my biggest adult fear. This fear fuelled my relentless pursuit of improvement, experiences, and growth. It also instilled a warped belief that material success was the only path to happiness. My entire life became a reflection of this relentless chase.

Ironically, my focus on achieving success and helping others, though intended to safeguard against abandonment, became self-protection. It wasn't a guarantee of rejection, after all. I had fallen into the trap of neglecting my happiness while focusing on external factors. It was only when I realised I needed to take responsibility for my well-being that I truly discovered it.

Happiness, I found, wasn't something to be chased. Once I stopped seeking it in external validation and achievements, happiness emerged as a beautiful by-product. I stopped pursuing it, and it found me.

Taking accountability for my physical and mental health became a cornerstone of my new journey. I finally accepted that external factors have limited control over happiness. True happiness came from within, and I needed to cultivate internal responsibility and self-compassion. As I came to trust the process of this life, the path to my mental well-being felt less daunting, like a gentle slope instead of a sheer cliff.

I confronted my negative self-beliefs and the patterns I had formed. I had deeply ingrained feelings of inadequacy, fear of failure, and rejection, as well as a desperate need for external validation. I was like a balloon, buffeted by the winds of expectations and external events. Each gust triggered a storm of anxieties within me.

Identifying these patterns empowered me to confront them and develop a more favourable self-image. Much of my pain and anxiety surrounding El's choices stemmed from my limiting beliefs. I craved control and feared appearing vulnerable by seeking help. This fear had kept me hiding my struggles, unable to accept my own limitations and seek support.

Finally, I began to grasp the truth – I couldn't control everything, and controlling everything wasn't protecting me from pain, anyway. It was only by letting go of this need for control and certainty that I could move towards happiness. Through this self-discovery, I identified and acknowledged my negative thought patterns. It became clear how profoundly they had affected my well-being throughout my life.

Beneath my confident facade, I had a deeply ingrained negativity. I used phrases like 'knowing my luck' as a crutch, a way to expect failure. Over time, these patterns became so entrenched they felt like an extension of me. I bent over backward to avoid failure, actively suppressing any trace of vulnerability. Admitting to the fear of rejection or even the simple wish to belong felt impossible and incredibly risky.

I now craved change.

It was clear I had to shatter that self-defeating pattern of repetitive thinking. It was a hamster wheel of negativity, a relentless cycle leading nowhere, and I wanted off!

Fear clouded my path forward, but I knew inaction wasn't an option. Stepping onto an alternative path, even with uncertain footing, felt essential. My journey revealed truths that were difficult and emotionally taxing. They felt unsettling, unfamiliar, and uncertain. Accepting them meant mapping out a new future, yet I realised I had to face the behaviours, habits, and emotions that kept me tied to the past. Did I truly want these patterns to define my future?

Through introspection and self-awareness practices, I challenged these ingrained patterns and cultivate a more positive self-image. I embarked on a journey to finally understand my emotions, finally learning to acknowledge and embrace them. I had a deep-seated yearning for something different, and I realised my repetitive behaviour patterns were producing the same frustrating outcomes, a cycle I needed to break.

As my counsellor told me, 'If you continue to do what you do, you will get what you have got!'

Internal conflict was a battle I had always avoided, resorting to various means of suppressing my emotions. Fear, a constant companion, stemmed primarily from the reactions I expected from others. I never sat down to unpack these feelings, leaving me a stranger even to myself. The true nature of some of my emotions remained a mystery.

These emotions, often accompanied by anxiety, a churning stomach, and a searing sense of rejection, felt disproportionate to the situation. The fear of rejection, a deeply rooted vine, amplified everything. My emotional breakdown, however painful, presented a unique opportunity for an overdue self-examination. It was time to delve deeper.

Ultimately, the potential for growth triumphed over the discomfort of stagnation. With unwavering support from loved ones, I persisted in exploring and dismantling the patterns I'd recognised. This journey of self-discovery led to a profound sense of emotional well-being. It also involved revising my personal beliefs, shedding those that no longer aligned with my needs.

Faced with my breakdown, I had accepted the need for change. Cultivating a positive mindset and embracing the present moment became priorities, even during challenging times, and I learned to minimise my concern about external judgements. This shift in perspective led to a greater sense of personal authenticity for me. And it yielded an inner peace and calmness I deeply cherish.

Those people or societies who do not approve of you will fall away, and you will make better ones, more joyful ones.

If you numb vulnerability, shame, or fear, you are numbing joy, happiness, and gratitude.

By concealing my vulnerability, shame, and fear, I had also held back positive emotions such as gladness, bliss, and gratefulness. This recognition sparked a conscious effort to embrace my full range of emotions, which I had deemed undesirable.

Previously, both personal and external pressures had pushed me to suppress vulnerability and sensitivity, leading to feelings of overwhelming shame when I 'failed' to meet those expectations. Now, I disregarded these pressures.

My healing journey continued as I learned to embrace my feelings. I welcomed them without judgement, allowing them to flow through me before releasing them. Slowly, I dissolved the limitations imposed by these emotions and embraced a new state of awareness, understanding, and gratitude.

This shift within me triggered a positive transformation in my thinking. My world changed for the better. It empowered me to take action, to tackle life's challenges with a sense of agency. My happiness was my responsibility, and I was ready to take ownership of it.

28

INVESTING IN GROWTH

My journey continued with a proactive approach to self-improvement. I engaged in practices like listening to inspirational podcasts, delving into personal development books, and studying meditation techniques. These efforts fostered a continuous optimistic outlook. As I appreciated the positive aspects of life, my gratitude deepened, and so did my happiness.

This sense of gratitude translated into increased overall well-being. No more under the influence of external circumstances, I embraced a more empowered approach. A sense of joy and bliss became the norm, supplanting the narrative that I was a victim of life's circumstances.

Today, I remain vigilant. I invite limiting beliefs and attitudes to the surface, allowing them a temporary presence before releasing them. My emotions are no longer something to outrun. Concerns about how others perceive or treat me no longer hold power over me. Prioritising self-awareness and emotional acceptance has liberated me from the fear of judgement and the desperate need for external validation. My worth and sense of belonging are no longer subject to negotiation with others.

One of my favourite quotes is from *Braving the Wilderness* by Brené Brown: 'Don't walk through the world looking for evidence that you don't belong because you'll always find it.'

I take full responsibility for my feelings. My reactions to El, others, and situations stem from my own emotions, not external forces. Happiness is a choice, and I no longer believe others have the power to dictate mine. When triggered, I now consciously choose my response, preventing my emotions from hijacking me and causing overreactions, as they always did in the past.

I acknowledge the impact of experiences on my reactions, but I understand they don't control my present.

I've cultivated a strong support network of individuals who prioritise my well-being. They offer genuine support when I ask for it – and I do ask now. This fosters belonging and connection while nurturing my personal autonomy and self-reliance.

Self-love is the foundation. When we cultivate love for ourselves, we gain the courage to face our fears. Forgiveness then becomes a natural consequence, even towards those who have hurt us.

29

MOMENTUM

I continued to heal, and a shift occurred within me, allowing me to view the world through a lens of positivity and appreciation. It was like emerging from a fog and seeing the world clearly for the first time. The beauty of a sunrise, a kind word from a stranger, even a simple cup of coffee – all these bring me joy. A new-found composure guides me through challenges. In simple terms, I have a better emotional state – content, happy, and peaceful.

Perhaps this sounds unusual, and that's perfectly all right. I share it because this change has been transformative.

I am no longer the frantic swan paddling beneath the surface while feigning calm. My journey has transformed me into a majestic swan, gliding gracefully across the still waters of existence. The reflections of challenges and emotions may disturb the surface, but I remain unruffled. I've embraced the flow, accepting emotions without judgement and letting go of rigid expectations. Yielding to the process, I undergo life's unfolding with tranquillity.

30

FUNDAMENTAL WELL-BEING

A year after El's second transitioning announcement and a year into my healing process, an unexpected wave of joy washed over me. It came without warning as I strolled alone through a shopping centre. The intensity of the emotion brought me to my knees. Lowering myself onto a bench, I shielded tear-filled eyes behind sunglasses – tears not of sadness but of pure, unadulterated joy. It was a euphoria unlike anything I'd ever known, an experience of complete well-being that absorbed me. I could not explain it. I only know I had a definite feeling of gratitude and that everything had changed. I left the shopping centre in a daze. I only remember looking around me at a place I had known for years and thinking, *Has it always been so beautiful here, and I just didn't notice?*

That memory remains a beacon, a constant reminder of the profound joy I discovered within myself. It was a transformation.

Although I haven't been able to duplicate that specific experience, a sense of calm and peace permeates my entire existence. I realised I had been striving to support El while grappling with an emotional state characterised by dissatisfaction and self-evaluation, but as I embraced this novel sentiment, I discovered freedom. Life's challenges haven't vanished – there are still days of frustration, anger, and low moods. However, I now embrace these emotions, allowing them temporary space before gently releasing them.

Even my kids have noticed. Their constant refrain, 'What's got into you, Mom? Can't you bottle that stuff?' is all the validation I need.

After years of mental gymnastics, the calm feels like a soothing balm. It's surreal to witness the transformation within myself. Concerns like finances, housing, world events, and friendships haven't vanished, but they no longer hold dominion over my happiness. For someone who craved control and certainty my entire life, this new freedom is a revelation. *Who is this person?* I ask myself, still marvelling at the transformation.

31

MANIFEST

My personal shift manifested in countless ways, most notably in my willingness to listen to my inner voice for the first time. It guided me to consider writing this book, a decision that would have been unthinkable in the past.

The seed of inspiration sprouted on a crisp winter run. I couldn't ignore the irony – I had always considered writing a realm that was off limits to me. Gaps in grammar and spelling, left by my education, coupled with a harsh inner critic to fuel my self-doubt. Yet the idea lingered, a persistent ember refusing to die in my subconscious.

Amid the wave of emotions tied to this idea, resistance surfaced first. The daunting task of writing a book sent me into retreat. But I couldn't ignore the concept. It returned like a recurring dream over a significant period. Finally, these insistent whispers compelled me to take a chance on this project.

Faced with my limitations, I explored outsourcing the work. Ghostwriters, those mythical story weavers, seemed like the answer. Surely they were the key to sharing El's story. However, a quick reality check – budget – quashed that dream faster than you could say 'bank balance'. Back to the drawing board – this time, for good measure, with a renewed sense that I wouldn't succeed.

Still, the urge to share this story, fuelled by a blossoming sense of purpose and fulfilment, refused to be silenced. My new calmness and inner wisdom instilled a quiet confidence – a belief in my ability to navigate this desire and bring the project to life.

Life had presented challenges before, and I'd conquered them, propelled by inspiration and a burning ambition. Why should this be any different? The persistent urge to share my story resonated with that same call to action – this time, driven not by external validation but by a deep sense of purpose and fulfilment. Finally, the whispers grew to a roar, impossible to ignore. With a deep breath and a surge of determination, I took action and began to write.

The journey wasn't without its roadblocks. Self-doubt slithered in with insidious lies: 'I can't do this.' In moments of discouragement, drafts deemed rubbish met their demise on the shelf. Yet with each setback, my determination solidified. I pressed on, and slowly, a clearer vision for the book crystallised. Each step forward brought the book's focus into sharper relief.

The prospect of sharing my initial draft with trusted friends ignited a familiar pang of vulnerability. However, my new inner peace acted as a shield. I acknowledged these emotions, processing them calmly. The feedback, a blend of constructive criticism and heart-warming encouragement, fed my motivation to continue the journey.

Emboldened by the positive feedback, I knew I couldn't succumb to fear any longer. Seeking professional help seemed like the next logical step. Financial limitations and the looming workload sparked a fresh wave of uncertainty, forcing a temporary pause. Yet the dream of sharing my story burned brightly, and I was adamant about finding a way forward.

Self-doubt, a persistent niggle, surfaced, but my resolve remained firm. The project pulsed with purpose, thrusting me forward. I embraced a fluid approach, letting the narrative unfold organically. It felt like trusting a flowing river, surrendering to its current. And as I surrendered, the missing pieces materialised. A supportive editor emerged, and the story blossomed under our collaborative efforts.

This approach unlocked a wellspring of memories and experiences, enriching the narrative as I incorporated them. While my initial vision may have evolved, ongoing reflection and refinement led to a final product, one that fulfilled its intended purpose.

I know some may critique my book, but by baring my journey and emotions with honesty, I've embraced the spirit of Brené Brown's *Daring Greatly*.

It's a story that transcends El's experience, weaving themes of love, resilience, and the profound bonds that connect us all. It's a chronicle of El's remarkable path, mirrored by my parallel voyage of self-discovery. Through laughter and tears, triumphs and setbacks, we've forged a path that may resonate with anyone who has ever navigated the complexities of family life. I'm proud of the individuals my children have become, and I hope our experiences offer valuable insights for anyone on a similar journey.

My purpose isn't to dictate opinions or prescribe a specific perspective on transgender individuals. I've moved beyond the need to convince or persuade others of my rightness. Instead, I offer a heartfelt glimpse into our family's journey, hoping to foster understanding and acceptance.

My children might raise an eyebrow at my new-found zest for life, perhaps wondering whether I've lost my marbles. Let me assure them (and you), I'm perfectly sane. (I hope.) What's changed is my perspective. Everyday experiences have taken on a new lustre, evoking a sense of wonder I hadn't felt before.

The vulnerability that once held me captive and the apprehension of rejection are distant memories. This new strength propels me forward, eager to embrace whatever challenges the future holds. It's a perspective rooted in the present, yet every experience, every stumble and triumph, has had a part in weaving the intricate tapestry of who I am today.

Making choices that align with my values brings a greater sense of fulfilment than always trying to satisfy others. Focusing solely on external validation can provide no more than fleeting satisfaction. This journey of self-discovery seems like a map guiding me towards unexplored territories, where I uncover new layers and fresh possibilities with every step.

Even during periods of high activity, I prioritise rituals that cultivate inner peace and keep me grounded in my values. Meditation, time spent in nature, and activities that foster mental clarity have become my anchors. These practices ensure I navigate busy stretches with calm and retain my well-being.

My path to well-being was forged in the crucible of adversity. While I wouldn't wish those life-altering events on anyone, they became the unexpected catalyst for my journey. The challenges I faced forced a necessary reckoning, a deep reflection that led to a profound shift within me. In hindsight, I recognise the profound gift these experiences, as difficult as they were, ultimately became. I cannot express how thankful I am for their influence in making me the person I am today.

I now navigate life compass in hand, my values and purpose guiding every step. My worth is no longer defined by my possessions or achievements. What matters most is the journey I take, not the opinions of others. But it's easy to slip into old, familiar habits when life's challenges dredge up past hurts.

Facing the reality of publishing this book brought back the familiar knot of fear in my stomach, a feeling I thought I'd left behind. I awoke to a stomach heavy as lead, a cold dread clinging to my insides like a shroud, the silence of the morning amplifying the feeling of unease. This sudden, intense physical response completely baffled me. My heart pounded a deafening rhythm against my ribs, a wild, chaotic beat that echoed the fear in my mind. The fear of rejection, failure, and judgement consumed my inner peace, leaving me feeling hollow and anxious; I went into flight mode. The feeling of being a fraud washed over me in a cold wave of self-doubt. It was a low point, born from the anticipation of something truly frightening – vulnerability.

I harshly criticised my regression, berating myself for the intense wave of overwhelming emotions. Slowly, through talks with El marked by moments of shared understanding and gentle encouragement, I felt better and saw my situation more clearly. The weight of potential rejection and vulnerability was palpable, a heavy cloak that had momentarily stifled me, yet I had acknowledged its presence. Instead of battling them, I allowed the unwelcome emotions to flow through me, their intensity slowly fading as the peace I longed for returned, a gentle silence replacing the inner turmoil. Finally, I let go of self-judgment, replacing the negativity with a sense of understanding and self-acceptance; it felt like a weight lifting off my chest.

No matter how well we believe we've conquered our inner demons, there will be times when those old, painful beliefs claw their way back into our consciousness, accompanied by a familiar knot of anxiety in the stomach. This was truly one of those moments in my life, a time I could feel the weight of the world. It demanded time for reflection, a grasp of the complexities involved, and the resilience to persevere through challenges. Facing my fear, I took a deep breath and dared greatly!

32

PRACTICES

Here are some practices I've incorporated to cultivate and maintain feelings of calmness that I hope will benefit other parents navigating similar journeys:

Practices for Inner Peace

Over the past several years, I've established a consistent routine that prioritises positive habits to support my overall well-being and inner peace. This routine includes regular exercise, healthy eating, and activities that promote positive feelings.

1. Embrace a Healthy Lifestyle

Maintaining a healthy lifestyle is a cornerstone of my well-being. Regular exercise has been a part of my routine for years, and I enjoy nourishing my body with nutritious home-cooked meals. While I might not be the life of the party when it comes to alcohol, I find other ways to unwind and relax (my friends can attest to my, shall we say, enthusiastic socialising skills after only two vinos!).

2. Cultivate Mind-Body Harmony

Reaching a state of true mental stillness proved to be a challenge, but practices like meditation, breathing exercises, and yoga have become valuable techniques. I've also found that appreciating the beauty in everyday moments grounds me and brings me peace. It's an ongoing process, but with consistent effort, I'm finding greater inner quiet.

3. Align Passion with Purpose

A key ingredient to well-being is finding joy in what you do. Whether it's a career aligned with your passions or hobbies that bring you immense pleasure, there's immense power in harmonising your activities with your values and interests. It's about finding fulfilment in the act of doing, not just chasing a pay cheque.

For me, this meant a significant life shift. I prioritised activities that sparked joy and fulfilment, like renovating my home and retraining to become a personal development coach. But the beauty lies in the universality of this principle. Finding fulfilment doesn't require a complete overhaul.

You can start by prioritising activities that match your values, like renovating a room, taking up painting, or spending quality time with loved ones. Even small actions, like spending time in nature or engaging in a creative hobby, can contribute to your overall well-being. Just make time for something that brings you joy.

4. Embrace the Flow

There's a certain peace in trusting your intuition and going with the flow. When you're guided by inspiration, purpose, and acceptance of what is, there is an incredible sense of liberation. It's about navigating life's currents with ease, taking the path of least resistance.

Life throws opportunities our way, sparking ideas, igniting creativity, and inspiring action. When these moments arise, it's valuable to engage with them. Set clear intentions, identify workable solutions, and trust your intuition as you navigate the process.

This approach has transformed my perspective. For me, it's about embracing a more relaxed and intuitive way of being in the world.

5. Exercise Self-Reflection

Self-reflection is a powerful tool for personal growth. It's allowed me to identify and manage unhelpful behaviour patterns, becoming more aware of triggers that might cause me to revert to old habits. When these moments arise, I approach them with self-compassion, focusing on developing alternative, more constructive responses. It takes practice, but over time, you become more aware and can self-correct.

Insights and Growth

Various informative resources and practices enriched my journey. Podcasts, with their thought-provoking content and fabulous meditations, played a significant role. These meditations offered valuable skills and techniques for calming my mind and fostering inner peace – some taking mere seconds to practise. As I learned to quiet my mind, a feeling of calm emerged.

Significant effort went into my personal growth, but the rewards have been immense. It was a critical component of my resilience and overcoming my challenges. This journey of understanding was a solo expedition, and reaching this point feels empowering. This emotional shift also significantly impacted my approach to El's second journey.

The fear for El and the worry about her choices were still present, of course. Old anxieties, like a shadow, sometimes crept back in. However, the sense of calm I'd cultivated now served as my anchor. Despite my fears for El, I could access that inner peace, allowing me to navigate El's second journey with greater strength, compassion, and understanding. Our perceptions shape our reality, and I began to examine the way I looked at things. As I adjusted my perspective, I began to feel less stressed and more open. My situation hadn't changed, but the way I looked at it had. That made all the difference.

In the words of Dr Wayne Dyer, 'Change the way you look at things, and the things you look at will change.'

PART THREE:

OUR JOURNEY

33

MOVING FORWARD

El again embarked on a journey of self-discovery, researching various medical transition options and seeking guidance from healthcare professionals. We consulted specialists and secured referrals through El's support network. To finance this process, we planned to leverage the equity in her home. El resumed hormone therapy, starting with a low dose of oestrogen, which accumulated before introducing a testosterone blocker.

While my anxieties about El's future resurfaced, my personal growth allowed me to stay positive and challenge fear-based thoughts. I participated in El's journey, attending appointments with El, now seeking information I previously avoided. While I wasn't yet conversant with transgender identity, I trusted El's self-knowledge and followed her lead.

Delays caused by a shortage of experienced professionals in transgender healthcare, resulting in frustratingly long waiting times for consultations and procedures, hindered El's enthusiasm for her medical transition. Nonetheless, we understood the importance of having a logical strategy. So we dug deep, researching and exploring every medical transition option available globally. Once again, El completed the assessments with her GP and therapist. Although she wasn't starting from scratch, she still had to re-establish her connections with both.

It's important to remember that not every transgender person chooses, or can afford, every medical intervention available. Media portrayals often suggest otherwise, creating a misconception that medical transitions are impulsive or readily accessible. In reality, the process in the UK, as in many places, involves lengthy waiting times and thorough assessments before a patient can access medical treatments. The sheer size of waiting lists in the UK debunks the myth of easy access.

In Britain, medical interventions are typically not available for individuals under eighteen. Young people who identify as transgender can, however, explore changes in their social presentation, such as name, pronouns, clothing choices, and hairstyles.

Sensation-driven media headlines often fuel misinformation about medical transition. It's essential to prioritise reliable sources over potentially misleading media narratives.

El's experience further emphasises the complexities involved for anyone transitioning. Contrary to inaccurate media portrayals, there are no immediate acceptances or fast-track options. El navigated challenging questions and considerations throughout her journey.

While cumbersome and repetitive, the initial professional assessments El underwent once again were crucial. They ensured she had a comprehensive understanding of the potential physical changes involved in medical transition. El needed to deliberate these outcomes and their impact on her body. For many transgender individuals, this process leads to a decision to forgo surgery; they find that living with gender dysphoria is their preferred path. This was never a consideration for El.

El's second journey, like her first, was fraught with challenges. Securing additional funds for FFS seemed impossible. With the ever-present fear of judgement, navigating work complexities added another layer of stress. These stressors accumulated over time, creating an invisible prison. The culmination of these pressures was evident in terrifying panic attacks that assaulted El during the night. Each one felt like a heart attack to El, who experienced difficulty breathing and a constricting pressure in her chest.

Coiling up in a ball in the bathroom with a window open gave El temporary relief, but it wasn't a permanent fix. We explored various coping mechanisms, including relaxation techniques and deep breathing exercises.

El had constructed a secret life, a world where her authentic self remained hidden at work. Fear of rejection, of whispers behind closed doors, and of a potential lack of understanding were the bars of the invisible cage she'd built around herself. The stress of maintaining this facade, coupled with the logistical hurdles of organising her transition, became a breeding ground for her panic attacks.

Finally, gathering her courage, El chose disclosure. Her anxiety was palpable, but to her immense relief, the response was overwhelmingly supportive. The panic attacks, though not entirely eradicated, lessened in intensity. A further advance loan on her house also arrived in her bank account, easing some of the financial burden.

With the financial hurdle cleared, El wasted no time in reigniting her efforts to obtain gender-affirming healthcare. She committed herself to taking concrete steps to live authentically as her true self. El's choices were personal, reflecting her unique journey.

She resumed hormone therapy through GenderGP and began laser treatment. Since she had already experienced puberty, puberty blockers weren't an option for her, but she grew her hair long again, dressed in a feminine way, and used she/her pronouns.

Puberty Blockers: A Brief Explanation

Puberty blockers are medications that can pause the physical changes of puberty. They are reversible and can allow adolescents experiencing gender dysphoria additional time for personal exploration and consideration of their gender identity. This allows puberty to resume if desired.

The long-term effects of puberty blockers on gender dysphoria are still being studied. Some researchers are investigating whether these medications might influence how gender dysphoria develops or resolves. While more research is needed to fully understand the potential effects, there is currently no firm evidence that puberty blockers cause gender dysphoria.

Puberty Blockers and Informed Consent

In 2020, an English court ordered the country's sole paediatric gender clinic to seek judicial approval before offering children puberty-blocking drugs. They concluded that minors cannot be competent to consent to treatment that will alter the rest of their lives.

However, in 2021, the Court of Appeal decided that it is for doctors, not judges, to decide whether individuals younger than sixteen with gender dysphoria can consent to treatment. They decided parents could provide consent to blockers on their behalf.

In 2022, NHS England's review commission revealed weak evidence regarding gender care and advised 'extreme caution' in prescribing puberty blockers. Disappointingly, the report neglected to include the positive experiences of trans children who had access to puberty blockers and falsely depicted trans children as traumatised, which is not true.

The report suggested a comprehensive evaluation of a child's needs, including screening for neurodevelopmental conditions like autism spectrum disorder, none of which El had. The report expressed the specific attitude that led to her deteriorating mental well-being. El wouldn't have benefited from any of the screening suggested; she simply required support for her transition. With access to puberty blockers, El might have avoided some of the most difficult aspects of puberty, such as the sudden increase in body hair and the dramatic change in her voice.

The prescription of puberty blockers for all trans children, except those in clinical research, was halted by this interim report.

The Gender Identity Development Service was the only NHS gender clinic for children in England and Wales. It closed in March 2024. It was replaced by the NHS Children and Young People's Gender Service, one in the North and one in London. We wait to see the effectiveness of these new clinics.

As a teacher, I agree children often try to fit in, bowing to peer pressure and trends. Important as it is to understand the social pressures young people face today, it's also crucial to recognise the unique experiences of transgender individuals. By confronting potential misunderstandings about gender identity through our education system, we can cultivate a more inclusive and supportive environment. We can, through these teachings, emphasise respect and awareness without minimising the complexities of individual journeys. We can then educate our young children about how transitioning is not something to be taken lightly or as a fashion option.

Still, today's government attempts to silence teachers and prevent them from creating what could be a safe place for many children.

34

ADULT GENDER TRANSITION

Navigating transition as an adult is a demanding and lengthy process, requiring resilience and determination to see it through. The decision for El to pursue her gender transitioning reflected a deep personal need and a willingness to face all potential difficulties.

Not all trans people wish to complete this journey. Some may choose alternative paths or find contentment in transitioning in some respects but not others, such as seeking only social or non-medical transition. Some individuals who transition experience regret or find their needs change.

Under the Gender Recognition Act 2004, UK adults can get a gender recognition certificate if they meet certain criteria. They must be eighteen or over, have a gender dysphoria diagnosis, provide evidence of living full-time in their self-identified gender for at least two years, and make a declaration that they will live permanently in their acquired gender, as well as paying a five-pound fee.

You do not need a gender recognition certificate to update your driving licence, passport, or legal documents, but you need one to update your birth, marriage, and death certificates.

Factors such as personal preferences, access to resources, and support systems can influence the choices individuals make in expressing their gender identity. Seeking guidance from qualified and affirming mental health professionals is invaluable in navigating the transition process and ensuring informed decision-making.

Finding a qualified mental health professional experienced in providing affirmative care for El was paramount. I had to know that El would get the best specialist care.

A qualified professional can also provide guidance and referrals to other helping professionals, but assessing support can involve significant waiting times for initial consultations. For El, this was often over six months; subsequent appointments with specialised care providers to attend the local gender clinic took over two years – and this was before Covid lengthened delays.

According to recent reports, waiting times have extended far beyond this. In England, NHS data shows that patients receiving first appointments in November 2023 had been waiting on average over seven years. The size of current waiting lists, together with the number of first appointments offered in 2023, suggest it would take at least ten years to clear the current appointment backlog, provided there were no changes to service provisions or waiting lists.

According to the latest available data, towards the end of 2023, over thirty-one thousand transgender people were on the waiting list for a first appointment at a gender identity clinic in England. So be prepared for these delays in the adult transition process.

El and I often faced long waiting times and poor communication from healthcare providers while we navigated the complex healthcare system, making an already arduous process even more frustrating and challenging for us both.

El diligently researched surgeons and consultants for her desired surgeries, exploring options beyond the UK because of the limited availability of experienced surgeons within budget constraints. I considered her choices and spent many hours supporting her through the decision-making process.

El's primary objective was to find highly skilled surgeons in her chosen field, considering her financial limitations. Mine was to ensure she received the procedure she chose, performed correctly by an experienced and reputable specialist.

El was always clear with me that she desired and would require medical intervention. She suffered from intense feelings of anxiety, distress, and unhappiness in relation to her primary sex characteristics (genitals) and secondary sex characteristics (chest, hair, voice). These feelings come under the umbrella of gender dysphoria, a term that acknowledges the distress some people experience because of a mismatch between their gender identity and their sex assigned at birth. (The term *gender identity disorder* is no longer used because of its potential to be seen as pathologising.) The ways people experience gender dysphoria vary, leading to diverse needs for support and potential treatment; I can share only my experience supporting my daughter through her journey. While El experienced gender dysphoria, it's essential to note that not all transgender people do. Its manifestation can also vary between individuals.

El said gender dysphoria was a visual thing for her and described it as 'overwhelmingly heartbreaking when looking in the mirror'. She was so uncomfortable with her body that she needed to change it. She felt constant pain and frustration at the mismatch between her physical body and her inner sense of self.

El identified concerns with certain facial features, as well as her facial hair. She managed her facial hair with laser hair removal and proactively consulted with several FFS specialists to explore the possibility of modifying other features to better align with her identity.

While I supported El through her FFS consultations, this triggered a wave of emotions in me, including anxieties about the potential impact on our relationship and the adjustments I might need to make. One significant fear was the potential loss of my identity as 'El's parent.' Would our bond change? How would I adjust to seeing El's physical presentation change? Would I know El if I passed her in the street?

In contrast with the way my old self would have dealt with these anxieties, this time, I communicated with El and her chosen professionals in order to navigate them and gain a better understanding of her perspective. El's chosen surgeons addressed my concerns by providing detailed information and offering reassurance. When I saw El's face in the first week after surgery, it pleasantly surprised me. While she looked different, I saw the same El, shining through in a way that deeply touched me.

El was thrilled with her surgeons, and I asked relevant questions about their reputation and experience at each session to ensure that I could fully support her. As El navigated her transition, I continued to deepen my understanding of her choices and her experience. However, I was still on my journey to fully grasp some aspects of it.

35

FACIAL FEMINISATION SURGERY

As part of the process of completing El's FFS surgeries, in 2022, we undertook several trips to Spain for consultations with her surgeons and a specialist therapist. El, now twenty-six, had already ruled out treatment in the UK because of long waiting times and the USA because of prohibitive costs, making Facialteam Marbella her preferred choice. However, she was worried about obtaining an appointment, knowing the wait could be up to six months or even a year.

In April, while I was already in Spain and El had time off, she called to tell me Facialteam Marbella had a cancellation for an initial consultation on the fourteenth. Surprised, I arranged a car rental for our ten-hour round trip to the FFS team in Marbella while El booked a flight into Alicante airport.

The five-hour drive to Marbella became a space for shared understanding. El, with new confidence, detailed her transition goals, the procedures involved, and the expected outcome. I, in a new-found state of acceptance, listened, eager to hear her perspective. El even commented on the shift in my demeanour, noticing a greater sense of calm in my approach to her journey.

The conversation naturally flowed to my own transformation. Fuelled by the recent inspiration from *Daring Greatly*, I found myself declaring solutions to challenges with a resounding 'Dare greatly!' El, unable to contain her amusement, threatened to immortalise my new motto on my tombstone. This light-hearted moment encapsulated the essence of my transformation – a shift towards acceptance and understanding, with a touch of humour along the way.

To break up the journey, we stayed overnight in a Puerto Banús apartment before continuing to Marbella. After arriving, now that I was off driving duty, I headed to the rooftop cocktail bar for a well-deserved cosmopolitan (or two). El hadn't joined me yet. As I sipped my second drink, a figure caught my eye. A wave of confusion washed over me. The woman in the flowing dress, her face with subtle make-up and her hair in cascading waves, couldn't be... El? But it was. And the joy radiating from her as she confidently walked towards me was undeniable. She looked amazing and deeply happy.

We had a great evening spending quality time with each other, and El's excitement for her appointment the next day was contagious. Together, we had started a years-long journey, and reaching this significant milestone filled me with relief and quiet pride.

A Mother's Concern

During our consultations, El's medical team spoke with me to address my concerns about pain management and recovery. They provided a comprehensive overview of El's post-operative care, including the recovery timeline and process.

The medical team explained the expected challenges El's nasal reconstruction would pose during the first twenty-four hours. I was against this procedure, as I didn't feel El needed it. They reassured me that things would become easier once the obstructions were removed. They outlined a gradual improvement over the following days, with the expectation that El would require only ibuprofen for pain management and would have minimal bruising by the time for our departing flight, which would take place two weeks after we arrived for the surgical procedures. The quick recovery timeline surprised me, but I hoped it would hold true for El. I was keeping everything crossed for her.

As I adjusted to the possibility of El's altered appearance after surgery, her vision for her journey remained unwavering. I respected her choices, even when they disagreed with mine. She remained steadfast despite the increased discomfort and my discouragement from some procedures. Some aspects of El's journey were unfamiliar, so I participated in consultations, positively adjusted my understanding, and supported her during this challenging phase.

To undertake surgical procedures in reputable establishments outside the UK, a referral letter from a qualified healthcare professional specialising in gender dysphoria is necessary. This is a prerequisite for accessing gender confirmation surgery. The referral process may involve assessments and confirmation of relevant treatment history. El obtained her referral letter via GenderGP.

Witnessing El's first and now her second journey often evoked a roller coaster of emotions in me. While I yearned for her happiness above all else, anxieties about her well-being and the success of her transition continued to trouble me. I worried that transitioning might not bring El the fulfilment and peace she desired, and this fear was always a constant, unspoken worry.

Questions like *What if this doesn't make her happy?* echoed in my mind, reflecting my deepest fear. Despite sometimes feeling overwhelmed with anxieties, I never wavered in my commitment to supporting El's choices. Regardless of my fear, I never stopped hoping for her happiness. But if I'm honest, even then, some part of me still hoped she might change her mind.

36

FFS OPERATIONS

Trans women who have gone through testosterone puberty may have undergone physical changes such as changes in voice pitch, facial and body hair growth, and obtaining a more muscular build. However, these experiences vary; El did not have a deep voice.

Quotes for FFS to rectify such changes can range from £10,000 to £50,000, including hospital and anaesthesia fees. The exact cost depends on the type and number of procedures needed to achieve the desired outcome, the surgeon's experience, and the geographic location. Some clinics or surgeons may offer financing options to help make FFS more affordable.

El chose Facialteam Marbella in Spain. Her chosen procedures were as follows:

Nose Feminisation Surgery with Rhinoplasty

Nose feminisation surgery, often combined with forehead reconstruction, creates a smooth transition between the forehead and nose (frontonasal transition). This procedure refines the nose by reducing its size, narrowing the bridge and width of the nostrils, and softening the tip. It's a common part of FFS and can help people experiencing gender dysphoria achieve a more balanced and feminine facial appearance.

Masculine noses are larger and wider than feminine noses, with a more prominent bone structure. The transition from forehead to nose is also sharper in men. Nose feminisation surgery addresses these features with rhinoplasty techniques to create a more delicate and balanced look.

This procedure caused a disagreement between El and me. I didn't think it was necessary to choose this procedure; her nose appeared perfectly fine to me. Graphic images and descriptions of the uncomfortable post-operative recovery from this procedure influenced me powerfully. The surgeon acknowledged it was an elective surgery but respected El's decision to go ahead with it. Consequently, I respected her choice, and we moved forward.

Forehead Feminisation

The brow ridge framing the eyes is a distinct gender marker. Male foreheads typically have more pronounced features overshadowing the eyes, contributing to a masculine appearance. In contrast, female foreheads are smoother, with less prominent brow bones. Interestingly, forehead height isn't the key difference; it's the hairline shape.

Techniques in Forehead Feminisation

Forehead feminisation, also known as forehead reduction surgery, achieves a smoother and more feminine appearance through a delicate balance of maxillofacial techniques. Bone osteotomies minimise bone volume and reduces brow ridge prominence, while bone burring sculpts the bone to further refine the brow ridge and create a smoother forehead shape.

Chin Feminisation Surgery

Chin feminisation surgery refers to various procedures that change the chin's position, shape, and volume – mentoplasty, contouring, and sliding genioplasty – to create a more balanced and feminine facial appearance. By adjusting the chin's height, width, and projection based on a patient's anatomy and desired results, these procedures achieve a natural-looking, feminine outcome. A well-defined chin improves the overall aesthetics of the lower jaw and chin region.

For El, no scars were caused by this surgery; the surgeons proceeded via the mouth.

Jaw Feminisation Surgery

Jaw feminisation surgery modifies the size of the jawbone to achieve a more feminine facial appearance. This involves reducing the jaw's height and volume through various bone sculpting techniques.

Jaw re-contouring can significantly change appearance. Procedures focus on three key areas: the angles, position, and volume of the lower jaw. Techniques are meticulously planned, ensuring precise adjustments to the width, height, projection, and volume of the jawbone. Depending on the desired outcome, a client may be offered jaw contouring procedures or osteotomies (bone segment removal), or even a combination of both. These procedures require complex surgical planning and expertise for successful outcomes.

Hair and Hairline Feminisation

Female hairlines have a rounded or smooth, slightly arched shape, positioned higher on the forehead compared to the typical M-shaped hairline in males. Women also have a more even distribution of hair density near the hairline. Of course, these are generalisations, and hairlines can vary among individuals.

Hairline feminisation can be a goal for some people seeking a more feminine facial appearance. As El had long flowing hair, any evidence of this procedure was well hidden from view.

Tracheal Shave

The laryngeal prominence, or Adam's apple, is a source of discomfort for some transgender women experiencing gender dysphoria. This protrusion can contribute to misgendering. A chondroplasty, or tracheal shave feminisation, is a common procedure in FFS, though not every transgender woman seeks this procedure. It can reduce the size of the laryngeal prominence, creating a smoother neck and throat contour that aligns with some goals of FFS. The procedure involves carefully removing a portion of the thyroid cartilage through a small incision under the chin.

The tiny scar caused by this procedure is amazing to see – or not see! Incredible.

37

FACIALTEAM MARBELLA

t was September 2022, and the time for the facial operations had arrived. We flew to Marbella for a two-week stay at the hospital. I stayed nearby, where I would be able to walk in everyday to visit El.

During the initial days, as El, still an outpatient, proceeded through all the pre-operative procedures and tests, we had chances to connect and share our perspectives. We cherished this quality time together, savouring delicious tapas at our favourite local restaurant, indulging in some well-deserved retail therapy, and exploring Marbella's Old Town. It was a time filled with gratitude for our connection and a hint of shared excitement for the journey ahead.

El settled in a hotel room in the charming Old Town of Marbella with its winding cobbled streets and abundance of unique restaurants and bars. After that, the team responsible for El's care after she left the hospital introduced themselves to us. Their attentiveness was heart-warming. They not only used the right pronouns when communicating with El but also went above and beyond to make her feel comfortable, such as by remembering her favourite drink and ensuring it was available in her room.

El took part in patient meetings, held several times a week, and connected with others at different stages of their journeys. The supportive environment encouraged her to ask questions freely. Witnessing the empathy and respect the team showed El, as when a nurse patiently addressed a concern using inclusive language and offering emotional support, left me incredibly relieved. I knew El had made the perfect choice in choosing Marbella to begin her medical transition.

During one uplifting conversation, we delved deep into El's feelings and her well-being over a delicious plate of parmigiana cheese pasta (always her favourite). While I was there to support her every step of the way, my own anxieties caused me to hesitantly bring up a lingering question: 'El, are you still sure about this? It's never too late to change your mind if you're having doubts.'

She understood this question stemmed from my concern as her mother, and with a smile, she reassured me that while she understood my worries, her commitment to her chosen path remained unwavering. *Okay,* I thought, *let's go, then. I am all in.*

After we'd spent an enjoyable few days in Marbella, a taxi took us to the hospital where El's procedures would take place. Facialteam Marbella operated within a beautifully landscaped hospital complex. Lush greenery, including towering trees and vibrant lawns, surrounded the building, while a sparkling pool added a touch of serenity to the setting. I was able to stay in this tranquil environment during my visits over the next few days. On some occasions, the surgeons would even join me for coffee and biscuits, offering friendly conversations and updates on El's progress.

We were escorted to her spacious first-floor room, a comfortable haven with a suite overlooking the hospital grounds. We unpacked her belongings and settled in, waiting for her dedicated nurse, Sarah, who would be with her twenty-four seven. Sarah also provided me with her mobile number in case it was necessary for me to discuss any concerns. The comprehensive care plan, comfortable environment, and readily available communication channels all contributed to a sense of calm and confidence, reassuring me of El's well-being during this important phase.

38

FFS OPERATION DAY

E l's surgery day arrived, and a knot of worry tightened in my stomach as I reached the hospital early. I settled El and left her in the capable hands of her nurses and surgeons. Afterward, I went shopping and for lunch at a beachfront restaurant I had seen earlier, attempting to distract my mind from worry. The day was hot, and the sun reflected off the still blue sea. It looked like a lovely holiday dream, but the dazzling scene in front of me didn't lift my mood as I stood by to hear from El.

The wait seemed unbearably lengthy. I took the long beach walk back to the hospital, hours too early, but I needed to be there, close to El. I felt relieved when I discovered the surgery itself had achieved success, but learning about the extended hair transplant procedure engendered fresh concern. El was in surgery for over eleven gruelling hours. Each procedure had gone to plan and there were no issues I had to worry about, but as I hadn't been able to physically see El, my worry did not dissipate. It was not possible for me to see her on that first day, but the option of connecting via phone that evening presented a glimmer of hope to my anxious heart.

While I would never have allowed El to go alone to Spain, this experience had its challenges for me. Being away from loved ones and in unfamiliar surroundings made it a lonely time. I remained positive and dug deep when I wavered, but panic still engulfed me as the enormousness of El's journey seized my mind and emotions. My stomach constantly churned with anxiety and worry. We had come so far, and it needed to be the right choice. In the back of my mind was the knowledge that some close to me still viewed El's transition as a choice rather than a necessity, which amplified my moments of loneliness. No one chooses these procedures; El had to do this to complete her journey.

Back at my apartment, El's call brought me a wave of relief as she told me she was doing well, although I wasn't quite convinced that evening. The night passed slowly, filled with anticipation and lingering worry. As dawn approached, I was up and preparing to head to the hospital when El called, her voice laced with discomfort and pain, and asked me to come quickly. Without hesitation, I rushed to her side.

Witnessing El's struggle in the first twenty-four hours was a challenge. Nausea from anaesthesia and nasal packing caused her significant discomfort. I watched anxiously, holding her hand and offering comfort. The hospital provided a bed, and I stayed by her side until she seemed more settled. I'd known this stage was going to be difficult, but I struggled to keep my emotions in check and stay positive for El. Several times, when she'd drifted back to sleep, I left her room to walk in the hospital grounds and allow my tears to fall. My heart ached. Each time, I took a deep breath, wiped my tears, and headed back to El's room.

I slept little in those twenty-four hours or the following morning; I braced myself for another challenging day. However, upon stepping into El's room, I encountered a delightful surprise. She rose, and her positive demeanour infused me with immense joy and relief. She was still in significant pain, but it was clear she had improved.

Witnessing her exceptional recovery progress over the next few days brought a significant shift in my emotional state. We relished simple pleasures like sharing stories over meals and short walks in the beautiful hospital gardens. Each day, her recovery progressed visibly, and the knot in my stomach slowly unravelled while the ache in my heart waned.

As El's FFS journey neared completion, a range of emotions overwhelmed me. Witnessing this transformation inspired awe and understanding. It created powerful moments of realisation and acceptance.

On the last day at the clinic, as I waited for El to return from her last procedure, the removal of her final nose bandage, the single moment as she came down the path solidified everything in my heart. She beamed, confidence radiating from her. This was the defining moment for me on El's journey. I now understood. This was right for El. I now had no doubts. I had gained a new understanding.

Only eight days post-surgery, El surprised me by venturing out for dinner. Even on the plane, with her sun hat and sunglasses, her minimal bruising and pain was manageable with ibuprofen. She looked so natural that I questioned whether anyone would suspect she'd had surgery.

As we travelled home, El looked different from her passport photo. Despite feeling uncomfortable about passport control, she'd decided not to change her picture until she finished her FFS. We'd received a letter from the facial team, confirming El's procedures, to help us during airport transitions if necessary. We passed through Spanish authorities without a backward glance, but UK border control was a different story. I cleared passport control and then turned around to wait for El. She stood at the counter, where the border control officer displayed obvious confusion. As I started walking back, searching my bag for the referral letter, I noticed El's smile. She concurred with the officer that her appearance no longer matched her photo. The officer smiled back and gestured for her to pass.

I travelled home that week with a different child. The peaceful aura around her was undeniable. I could not refrain from gazing at El, observing her confidence and joy. It filled me with immense happiness. The weight I had carried for nearly ten years finally lifted. I had often dreamed of this moment, when all the pain and worry would be behind us, and I couldn't believe it had arrived. We had done it! El was on her way to finding peace and happiness.

I realised at that moment that I hadn't lost a son or gained a daughter; my child had blossomed into the beautiful person they were always meant to be.

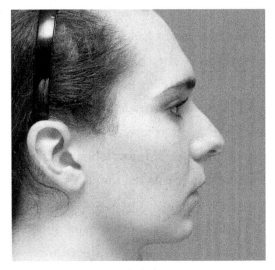

El's profile before FFS

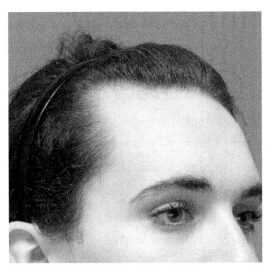

El's hairline before FFS

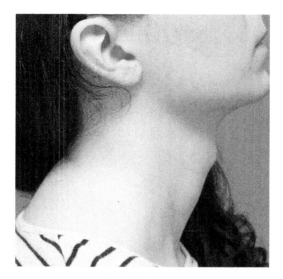

El's neck before FFS

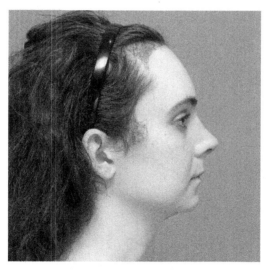

El's profile after FFS

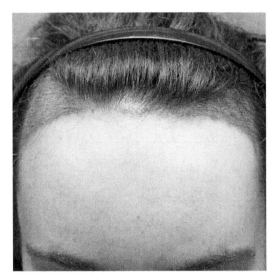

El's hairline after FFS

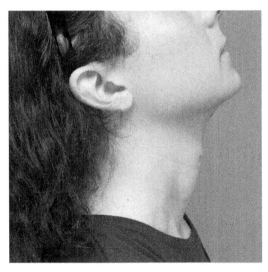

El's neck after FFS

El eight days after FFS

El twelve months after FFS, with the swelling and bruising gone

39

FAMILY DYNAMICS

During El's stay in Marbella, I interacted with several transgender adults undergoing similar procedures. The supportive atmosphere warmed my heart, and El thrived in it, although I know she still had moments of loneliness. Despite this, I couldn't escape the fact that I was the solitary parent in attendance. This made me wonder about the experiences of other families on this journey. There were other children without parental support during this transformative experience. It was heartbreaking.

These reflections triggered a wave of self-examination. Why had I not interacted with other parents before? Perhaps a part of me had clung to the hope that El wouldn't need to transition, leading me to disconnect from others on this journey. While I had been physically and financially present for El, I had also struggled to accept her journey. I'd harboured a small hope that this wouldn't happen.

When I thought back on my experience, I realised that there were extra support resources I could have used. Connecting with other parents might have provided valuable insights and connections, perhaps making my journey easier – and definitely less lonely.

Sharing this personal story has been a positive step for me, a cleansing experience that has allowed me to process and release some of the complex emotions I had surrounding El's transition. However difficult it was at times, I never regret being there every day for El in whatever capacity I could muster.

HOMECOMING

We arrived home from Spain, and the difference in my daughter shone through. With her medical team's approval, I booked her breast augmentation in six weeks, followed by a six-month break before the final surgery. Love replaced fear, and my focus shifted towards unwavering support and a hopeful future.

In the wake of this transformative experience, we set off on a new adventure together. Witnessing her confidence and excitement as we explored options filled me with immense pride and joy. We collaborated to choose new clothes and hairstyles that accentuated her natural beauty. It was a joyful time of self-discovery and shared support.

Christmas gift shopping included clothes and shoes. El's natural hair, which had now grown back, was long, thick, and curly – something most women would envy – and served as the basis for our experimentation with new hairstyles.

We pressed on, united in our conviction about this path. El's journey wasn't just hers; it was ours. The act of openly communicating her experiences solidified our shared commitment to supporting one another as we both explored unfamiliar territory. External opinions mattered less and less now as our focus shifted solely to El's well-being and happiness.

Her determination and confidence remained a constant source of inspiration. Watching her blossom filled me with a pride that went beyond words. El's journey wasn't just a medical transformation; it was a show of the strong, radiant woman she was always meant to be. It marked the beginning of a brand-new chapter, one where my sole concern remained her happiness.

My fears had given way to optimism, profound love, and admiration for the daughter I now saw before me. I saw a brave, strong, and fearless person who was prepared to face the challenges ahead to complete her transformation, and I was in awe of her.

With my optimism for El's future, I sold the family home and downsized to help finance the remaining surgeries for El to continue her transition. Gender realignment in the UK cost around £25,000 and was not accessible through the NHS.

The act of finding a buyer for our home was a pivotal moment for me. Over the years, I had poured my heart and soul into renovations, creating a space I was immensely proud of. Sanding every surface, painting every room, and landscaping the grounds – it was a testament to my efforts and a source of external validation.

However, now that I had re-evaluated my priorities, my definition of fulfilment had shifted. Once the house had been a symbol of outward success; now, selling it became a simple decision. The For Sale sign wasn't an ending; it was the start of a new chapter, built on internal validation and unwavering love for my child.

The process of selling our home to support El's journey was unexpectedly complex. The sale failed five times before it eventually sold. To ensure stability during this time, I opted for a temporary rental solution while continuing to hunt for a permanent residence that fitted my needs. Renting seemed undesirable to me, but since I hadn't come across a suitable house to buy, I reluctantly came to terms with it.

The search for temporary housing also presented unforeseen challenges. With limited time remaining, the situation felt precarious. Fortunately, a suitable property with ample storage became available with only five days remaining before completion of the sale. It was a close call, but a welcome resolution.

While the concept of renting didn't initially appeal to me, the situation presented a much-needed opportunity for individual growth and creating shared memories for me and El. This time allowed me to re-engage in activities I enjoyed, such as walking, jogging, reading, and relaxing in nature. It was a period of self-care that proved to be a crucial part of my healing journey and a great opportunity to spend quality time with El.

I spent over a year house-hunting, picturing myself curled up with a good book in a cosy nook or enjoying quiet mornings on a sunny patio. I toured countless places, some charming, some modern, but none felt quite right. That gut feeling that tells you 'this is the one' was always absent. Discouragement crept in, making me wonder if I'd ever find a place to call home again.

I remembered viewing a house in 2015 that I'd nearly bought, but the kids still lived with me, so I'd felt it was a bit small and bought a different property.

Fast-forward to 2022, when, just before leaving on holiday, I drove past the same house again. An inexplicable pull drew me to it, and I said aloud, 'That would be just perfect.'

Imagine my surprise when just four days later, while relaxing on the beach, I saw the very same house pop up on a property website! My eyes couldn't believe it, so I had to look again. I wasted no time scheduling a viewing, and despite competition from other offers, some even higher than mine, the seller accepted my offer.

Steeped in history, the 1777 Grade II listed stone cottage captivated me with its large sash windows and original features. Tucked away in a private courtyard within a charming village, it sat just steps from a friendly local pub. While restoration would be a labour of love, I envisioned bringing this piece of history back to its former glory. The project would necessitate commitment, but the potential for restoration was unquestionable. Not just a house but a canvas for creation stood before me. Restoring this historic gem promised not only satisfaction but an opportunity for me to do what gave me joy.

My relocation presented its fair share of difficulties, yet the sheer delight of locating my ideal sanctuary overshadowed the inconvenience and temporary hassle of renting. I entered my new home with a profound feeling of familiarity. The house resonated with my soul, offering a sense of peace and belonging I hadn't expected.

This experience was a beautiful reminder to stay open to possibilities and trust, synchronising with life's unfolding. The stars seemed to have aligned, and the timing couldn't have been more perfect. What can I say? I love it. It is my forever home. It appears as though destiny brought it to me, but only when the timing was right!

Selling our home provoked a variety of responses. I received both understanding and criticism for the choices I made to support El. While some individuals questioned the necessity or validity of her journey, calling the surgeries cosmetic and elective, I remained committed to providing support.

El, however, received unwavering support from her close-knit group of friends and her sister, Josie. This support encompassed practical help, emotional encouragement, and a strong sense of belonging. Josie, ever the supportive sister, offered make-up and fashion advice, helping El navigate her new style with confidence. She was a constant source of encouragement, celebrating El's triumphs throughout her journey and showering her with love.

El's father's offer of support towards her last operation especially touched her. This willingness from her father to become involved marked a significant shift in their dynamic, and they began rebuilding their relationship on a foundation of mutual understanding and acceptance. It continues to strengthen and flourish.

41

BREAST AUGMENTATION

Breast augmentation surgery is a procedure to increase the breast size. For transgender women, enhancing the breasts' fullness and projection provides a more feminine appearance.

El's breast augmentation was an outpatient surgery performed in London. After completing the initial consultation and getting El's required referral documentation, we travelled to London for the procedure. We travelled down in the morning and I left her at the clinic, ready to return later that day. Once again, I busied myself with shopping and visiting cafes to fill my mind with distracting thoughts while I waited for news on El. I headed back to the clinic in good time to see El and talk with her elected surgeon. All seemed to go well, and we drove home that night.

El stayed with me during her recovery period, as I worked from home and could look after her. My mind was filled with unease as I watched El grapple with the post-op recovery from this procedure. Her recovery was not following the path specified to us by the clinic, and El was in great discomfort and pain. She struggled to breathe, was lethargic, and wasn't eating. After a few days with only minor improvement, El contacted the clinic, which arranged an appointment with a consultant in our hometown.

The consultation resulted in the discovery of a blood clot. During surgery, the surgeon had snagged a blood vessel, causing El to develop a blood clot in her chest. Having faced a similar health concern in the past, I recognised the potential severity and experienced a surge of worry. I confess I went into panic mode.

It was not a rare or life-threatening complication. The situation required close monitoring and additional medical intervention. El was scheduled for surgery the next morning. She continued to struggle with pain in her chest and breathing, making it a long, challenging night for everyone involved.

We left early in the morning, after very little sleep, for the clinic in London. While the initial plan was based on a same-day discharge, the medical team kept El in for additional monitoring because of concerns about her resting heart rate. I found a hotel – difficult, as it was a Friday night in late December, and office Christmas parties were in full swing.

While El received further monitoring at the clinic, I took some time for myself. The festive lights offered a temporary distraction, and I located a quiet space to gather my thoughts. During this brief respite I connected with El, and her reassurance provided much-needed comfort. While I was relieved by her progress, the emotional weight of the past period began to settle in. I had travelled this journey alone with El for a long time. Tonight, in the cold winter, I had no toothbrush, clothes, or companion. I was tearful and tired.

I drove to pick El up in the morning and thanked the surgeon for the corrective procedure. El seemed much improved. Once home, she recovered quickly and was fully healed by Christmas.

FAMILY REUNION

The year of the FFS and breast operations, El and I joined my sister's family for Christmas. Spending the holidays with my sister felt like a welcome change after a year filled with treatments, appointments, and procedures. El and I both relished the prospect of a relaxed Christmas celebration, free from the usual holiday hustle and bustle.

The upcoming family gathering presented an opportunity for El and me to reconnect with our extended family. Both of us were experiencing pre-visit nerves. This would be the first time the rest of the family would see El since she had again begun her transition, and we had kept to ourselves since then. El, understandably, felt nervous, and I shared her apprehension.

Josie helped us choose a dress for El for Christmas. It was a beautiful feminine style, worn with boots and tights, and El seemed happy with the choice, but I was aware this was far removed from her last appearance with the family.

I had informed the family about El's journey, and while some may have had reservations, they were all welcoming and made a genuine effort to make El feel comfortable. Throughout the gathering, they engaged her in conversation, used her preferred name and pronouns, and offered her support and understanding.

The family gathering provided a welcome opportunity for reconnection, especially for El. Despite some initial anxieties, we experienced a day filled with warm welcomes, heartfelt conversations, and a shared sense of joy. It was a stirring reminder of the importance of family and the power of acceptance.

43

GENDER CONFIRMATION

El's journey throughout 2022 and 2023 was one of incredible growth and transformation. In August 2023, she would return home after completing her final gender confirmation surgery. While researching suitable surgeons together, I hesitated to delve into the intricacies. The finer details of the procedure were emotionally challenging. While I intellectually supported El's decision, part of me couldn't bear to imagine the painful recovery she would face.

About Gender Confirmation Surgery

Gender confirmation surgery, also known as gender-affirming surgery, is a medical procedure or series of procedures that allows transgender individuals to change their physical appearance to better align with their identified gender. This can involve a variety of procedures, including chest reconstruction, facial feminisation/masculinisation surgery, and genital surgeries such as vaginoplasty or phalloplasty. Gender confirmation surgery for trans women can include the removal of the testes (orchidectomy), removal of the penis (penectomy), construction of a vagina (vaginoplasty), construction of labia (labiaplasty), and construction of a clitoris (clitoroplasty).

Before undergoing any surgery, patients engage in hormone replacement therapy and may consider additional procedures such as hair removal. It's necessary to consult with a qualified healthcare professional to discuss individual needs and options.

In July 2023, El embarked on the final stage of her journey, gender confirmation surgery, opting for her partner's presence for this crucial moment rather than me, her mother. Blossoming in her relationship, she discussed her desire to have her partner by her side, and I wholeheartedly supported her choice. Ten years on from that fun-filled night, their introduction had blossomed into friendship and then love. Witnessing the fondness and encouragement they shared then and still share today fills me with immense joy. El's happiness is paramount, and I am thrilled for her and the future they are building together.

El's surgery took place in Thailand over a fourteen-day stay. Including accommodation for her and her partner, it cost approximately £18,000, excluding flights. A rigorous evaluation process, including getting a referral letter from her UK gender therapist, ensured she made an informed decision and received the best possible care from her chosen surgeon.

Once they arrived in Thailand, El's partner set up a WhatsApp group so that Josie, their dad, and I could follow her progress. They left for Thailand on 18 July and spent the first few days undergoing pre-operative tests and assessments, culminating in the procedure on 22 July. El celebrated her twenty-eighth birthday in Thailand on 28 July 2023. She had been travelling on this road for over ten years, and reaching twenty-eight gifted El the best present she could wish for.

I travelled down to Heathrow in early August to collect El and her partner, I was thrilled as I saw El walking towards me, supported by her partner and the case trolley.

On the journey home, El was obviously excited with how things had gone, and despite her physical discomfort at this stage, she was already planning future travels and activities

with her partner. She beamed with happiness and relief that she had obtained a body that matched her true gender identity. Her journey was now complete.

El and her partner two days after surgery.

THE FINAL STEP

As expected, recovery from El's gender confirmation surgery, the final stage of her journey, was the most demanding. She completed her transition in July 2023 but remained on medical leave from her physically demanding job until January 2024.

While El's FFS was a longer procedure, at eleven hours, the six-hour gender confirmation surgery presented a unique set of challenges requiring a longer recovery period. El struggled with physical activity for many months and had to delay her return to work due to continued discomfort and insufficient energy to complete a day's work. Undeterred, El discussed a phased return with her employer and embarked on a three-month programme to return to her workplace.

El's successful transition back to full-time work was facilitated by her employer, who played a crucial role in providing El with a flexible and supportive work environment.

El's employer accommodated flexible hours and days that changed from week to week based on El's well-being.

THE ENDGAME

Witnessing El's journey has been remarkable. Her personal growth has fostered an even greater sense of compassion and kindness towards others. She embraces individuality and approaches life with unwavering confidence. This transformative experience has brought her immense peace and self-acceptance, allowing her to embrace who she truly is. It has eased her psychological pain. Her heart no longer breaks when she looks in the mirror.

Despite some around her being unkind and thoughtless, and despite her temporary U-turn, she held fast and straight on her journey. Hers has been a journey of remarkable strength and perseverance. Despite encountering challenges and moments of doubt, she remained true to herself and her path. El has discovered her authentic self, and her resulting sense of peace and fulfilment is inspiring.

They say life begins when you leave your comfort zone, and boy, did El leave hers! She did indeed 'dare greatly'.

El's story highlights the importance of understanding and respecting individual journeys. While experiences can vary and some may face challenges or regrets, it's vital to promote supportive environments where personal growth and self-discovery can flourish. Ultimately, fostering a climate of acceptance allows individuals to make informed choices that align with their authentic selves. El's journey has affected my understanding of identity and the value of unwavering support, despite how difficult it may be.

El navigated her transition process with quiet determination and self-reliance, financing it independently (with a little help from Mum and Dad). While embarking on our second journey, I suggested she consider adding herself to the NHS waiting list for gender reassignment surgery, despite the long waiting times. El had demonstrably fulfilled the requirements for the programme. However, El ultimately pursued a private option to expedite her journey.

El says, 'While I understand the limitations of the waiting list, I couldn't bear the thought of occupying a spot that others desperately need, especially those who may face financial challenges in accessing this surgery through the public system. Contributing to the waiting times, which can be emotionally taxing for individuals, wouldn't sit right with me. It may have required hard work and additional support from my family, but for me, pursuing a private option was the right choice.'

That blew me away.

El's decision to self-fund her surgery was a significant step in her journey, driven by her personal goals and unwavering commitment. Her decision, a deeply personal one, reflected her values and priorities.

PERSONAL VALUES
AND CHOICES

I am not an advocate of rigid laws and regulations to define how people should believe or think. Understanding diverse perspectives allows us to create a more inclusive and supportive world. Though navigating these topics can be challenging, maintaining open communication, empathy, flexibility, and compassion is crucial.

El's journey has been a lesson in acceptance and respect for individual experiences. We should allow people to live according to the dictates of their religion or upbringing as long as they do not harm others who choose to live differently. Everyone deserves to live authentically, and open hearts lead to stronger connections. Those who transition should also accept that not all will agree with their choices, and that's okay too.

For me and El, it's about compassionate concessions that allow a minority to live in safety and dignity. A liberal society can accommodate many subjective beliefs, even mutually contradictory ones. Whether transitioning makes people happy is a question for the individual. And if transitioning makes the individual happy, then the question of whether gender-related ideologies are correct or whether all have to agree on them is, I believe, irrelevant.

Witnessing El's transformation has been an enriching experience. Her journey has helped both of us foster a deeper understanding, prizing compassion, empathy, and respect for individual choices. It's reminded me that personal happiness and authenticity are a fundamental right for everyone.

El desires to live her life as a transgender woman, to have the freedom to work without fear, to change her name, and to have the option of marrying and adopting children should she wish. Despite her choice, she does not anticipate everyone agreeing with or comprehending it. She just asks for tolerance and the ability to live life freely and without fear.

El has completed her journey and her external sexual organs, facial features, and body match those of other females. Through her transition, she has embraced her authentic identity as a woman. This necessitates the fundamental right to access facilities and services designated for women, ensuring her safety and dignity.

47

DETRANSITIONERS
AND DESISTERS

While El's path has been filled with personal growth and realisation, we must acknowledge the complexities surrounding gender identity and respect the diverse experiences of all individuals, including those who detransition.

A detransitioner is an individual who formerly identified as transgender.

A desister is someone who previously identified as transgender but who, prior to any medical intervention, re-identified with the gender assigned to them at birth. Prior to re-identifying with their assigned gender, many desisters underwent some social transition, which may include a change of name, pronouns, clothes, hairstyle, or other modifications to their appearance so they could express their gender identity.

The number of people who do not continue with transition varies depending on where in the world they live. It is subject to several factors, including societal acceptance of transgender people and access to healthcare. A tiny percentage of transgender individuals detransition, and the primary cause is usually lack of social acceptance, whether in the workplace; at home, work, or school; or with family or friends.

Detransitioning is a personal and often painful experience.

Although the number who detransition is low, it's easy to find detransition stories online, and they can be heartbreaking. Detransitioners should be treated with the respect they deserve, not vilified as transphobic. Their stories are painful, with some suffering irreparable loss, and it takes courage to speak out. We should applaud them for doing so. Their bravery allows transgender individuals, their parents, and other interested parties to gain a more balanced outlook while researching potential options, and all opinions and experiences here are valuable in providing a comprehensive picture.

We should not celebrate one group and silence another. Again, compassion and understanding are all that is required. Increased visibility and acceptance of transgender people can create a more inclusive environment, potentially reducing the number of future detransitioners.

48

BEING TRANSGENDER TODAY

El's journey to live authentically as herself has been remarkable. There were moments when she faced resistance, but her unwavering determination to live as the woman she knew she always has been was truly inspiring to me. Her courage in the face of adversity is something I will always admire. How many of us possess the bravery to embark on this journey and embrace the life we were meant to live? El is the bravest person I know.

Family and friends don't talk about El being transgender now. She is just El. El is navigating the legal aspects of her transition, including updating her name and documents. It's a significant step for her. No doubt we will encounter difficulties and delays in obtaining these documents, but we will prevail.

We are lucky to live in a country where El can live the life she chooses. I vividly remember her relief when she could finally access the healthcare she needed to transition. It's moments like these that make me grateful for the progress we've made here towards achieving LGBTQ+ rights, but it also underscores the fight for equality that continues in many parts of the world.

However, the lack of NHS support for treatment of transgender individuals is a cause for concern. Witnessing the struggles of others seeking treatment only strengthens my resolve to advocate for a more inclusive and supportive healthcare system.

The current state of access to gender-related healthcare in the UK raises many concerns. Many transgender individuals, including El, feel a sense of vulnerability and lack of support during a critical period in their journey because of the extended waiting times for NHS treatment. Many people still believe this support should not be given via the NHS in any shape or form, as funding comes from the public purse, and some would wish harm to my child. Debate continues on the rights of transgender adults in areas of marriage, sports, and the workplace – even whether they should be allowed to use public toilets.

I understand and accept some concerns raised. The issue of transgender people in sports is complex, and there's no straightforward solution. El and I share concerns about fairness in women's sports. Discovering a solution that upholds the rights of transgender athletes while maintaining fair competition for all female participants is essential. Female athletes have spent years working and training for their moment, and to be beaten by stronger, heavier, faster trans woman is going to give rise to frustration and anger. The debate over these issues has resulted in a ban on trans women participating as females in some sports.

In a 2023 statement, UK Athletics declared, "If your gender is different from the sex you were observed at birth, you are not allowed to compete in the female category from 1 April 2023 unless you are approved by UK Athletics as complying with the World Athletics Regulations." Transgender women athletes who were previously approved to compete through the UK Athletics panel process could no longer participate in the female category from 1 April, regardless of testosterone levels.

England Athletics stated, "If you have already registered to enter an event before midnight on 31 March 2023, you will be able to compete in that event but cannot claim awards, qualifying times or records. Your score will not count towards a team result."

Other national governing bodies, such as the Rugby Football Union and British Cycling, have gone further and stated that anyone who has gone through male puberty may not compete in female sport.

In our society, as in many others, people often misunderstand what it means to be transgender, and this ignorance can lead them to be unsupportive and unaccepting.

The recent misleading reports and media sensationalism surrounding two female boxers in the 2024 Paris Olympics, filled with exaggerated claims and biased perspectives, was a prime example. The media's false labelling of these two women, who were born female, as transgender fuelled fear and spread dangerous misinformation. This harmful narrative unfairly targets both trans athletes and cis women, unjustly questioning their rightful place in sports and diminishing their accomplishments. If a woman excels in her field, does that give others the right to doubt her biological sex?

I believe the harm I would have inflicted on my daughter had I chosen not to support her would have resulted in irreparable damage to El and to our relationship. Many young transgender people who suppress their true selves do so because of a lack of understanding and acceptance, leading to long-term harm. I hope and pray that we progress in the right direction, reducing the pain, fear, and anxiety faced by many transgender individuals.

I hope sharing El's journey highlights the value of support. It's been rewarding to witness the positive impact on her mental health that using her chosen name everywhere has had. This reinforces research that shows social acceptance and affirmation can significantly reduce depression and suicidal ideation in transgender youths.

By using chosen names and offering acceptance, we can improve our children's mental health outcomes. This support yields tremendous results for such little effort, reducing negative thoughts, anxiety, and shame among trans children with a simple show of acceptance. Surely that's the least we can do.

It's heartbreaking to hear stories of young people facing rejection and hostility from their families and communities just for being themselves. I've heard accounts of young trans adults being thrown out of their homes and choosing homelessness over a hostel or bed and breakfast that accepts only their birth gender. They fear being abused in one and beaten up in another.

No one, regardless of identity or sexual orientation, deserves to experience homelessness or fear abuse because of who they are.

Nobody should kick someone out of their social community or home because their identity lies somewhere on the LGBTQ+ spectrum. Everyone deserves love, and to give it is our natural state. Hate and anger are so much more exhausting. Let's all strive to create a world where every young person feels safe to be themselves.

A growing recognition of gender variance has led to greater visibility for transgender people. However, discrimination, harassment, and violence against the trans community remain prevalent globally. This is too often reported on our TV screens. Trans people remain unfamiliar to the average person, and therefore too many of us rely on media representation or political stances to understand this minority group.

Representing transgender people responsibly in the media and fostering empathy are crucial in creating a safer and more inclusive environment. And while media representation can play a role, it's essential to go beyond headlines and seek a genuine understanding of the lived experiences of transgender individuals.

WORK

Despite some progress, transgender people can still face persistent discrimination in the workplace, and transitioning can be a trigger for discrimination.

Though workplace discrimination remains commonplace, El has been fortunate to have worked for the last three years at a small and supportive company. Previously, during her first transitioning journey, El worked in the customer service department at a large supermarket chain and received some positive support from the company. She was open about her journey with close colleagues but preferred to blend in and avoid unnecessary attention.

However, El's career development within the supermarket chain stalled after she transitioned. While El perceived this as a potential consequence of her transition, the company never specified the reason for the halted advancement, making it impossible to connect the two events. She saw the manager less and less and then not at all. She felt like management marginalised her because of her transitioning, but it was impossible to prove. El subsequently resigned from her position.

Lucky as she has been in recent years, El has still felt the sting of workplace discrimination. One day, a confident trans woman entered the store where El worked, radiating self-acceptance. El's moment of inspiration was shattered by the cruel mockery she overheard from colleagues who ridiculed the woman's appearance and used the wrong pronouns. El's heart pounded with anger and disbelief at their insensitivity. *How could they be so cruel?* she wondered. Here was this woman, expressing herself, and they were tearing her down with their insensitive remarks.

The incident sparked an internal conflict in El. Her colleagues' mumbled apologies and the offhand remark 'It's different for you, you're acceptable' left a deep mark. Was her decision to keep her identity private a betrayal of the transgender community? The dissonance between El's admiration and her colleagues' mockery was stark, a blunt reminder of the prejudice that still existed in the world.

El understands the fear of rejection and discrimination remains very real, as are the challenges many face in the workplace.

Some individuals, including employers, might lack prior experience or understanding of transgender identities. This can create challenges in providing adequate support and fostering inclusive environments. Resources and guidance from organisations like the Government Equalities Office can be valuable in navigating these complexities.

During El's brief stint in the care industry – one of her first jobs, when she had recently begun dressing as a woman in public, had begun hormone treatment, and had changed her name from Billy to El – her dedication to her caregiving duties was constantly challenged by the arbitrary restrictions placed upon her. The most frustrating aspect was the inability to assist female residents with personal needs. It felt illogical, a contradiction to the very essence of caregiving. Here she was, trained and capable, yet societal norms dictated who she could and could not help.

El found these assumptions frustrating, but as a new member of the team, she kept her frustrations private.

El's work experience throughout her second transitioning has been positive. Her colleagues have provided encouragement, and management offered flexibility during her medical transition. The presence of support and understanding from her colleagues and management during this crucial phase was priceless and had a substantial impact on her well-being.

50

SUPPORTING YOUR TRANSGENDER CHILD

Being transgender in the UK remains challenging, and in my profession, I frequently encounter individuals seeking advice. Consequently, I have identified a handful of recommendations that may benefit those with a transgender child or other loved one.

Be Prepared for Change

Accepting and understanding your child's gender identity can bring about a transformation. Some friendships might change, while others may deepen. You may encounter negativity from people who believe you're doing the wrong thing. The most important thing to remember is that your child is not making a choice.

Create a Safe Space

Your child needs a safe and supportive environment to thrive. Find a community of friends who can provide wit, laughter, and hope in the face of the hostility and unkindness that society may show you.

Carve out a haven, wherever that is or whatever it looks like, for you and your child, away from negative attitudes. Forget your negative thoughts; they serve no purpose.

You may encounter challenges and negativity, whether from society or those close to you. But it's important to remember that you are not alone. Uncovering a community of friends who offer support, understanding, and acceptance is essential. Seek individuals who appreciate your child's genuine identity, establishing an environment where they can truly fit in. Remember, belonging doesn't require changing who you are; it's about embracing your true self and finding those who hold space for you and your boundaries.

Educate Yourself and Embrace Growth

Educate yourself as best you can and accept your feelings, negative or positive. Watch videos; read books. While I've had moments of uncertainty and negativity, I've come to embrace them as part of my growth process. In retrospect, I regret not seeking resources and connection within the local LGBTQ+ community earlier. I believe I would have gained valuable support and understanding.

As parents, it's important we remember that our child being transgender is not our fault. You are not to blame. We can't make our children transgender, and we can't stop them from being who they truly are. If your child isn't transgender, there is nothing you can do to make them transgender, and if they are transgender, it's not something you can change. Our role is to love and support them unconditionally on their unique journeys.

Love and Support Unconditionally

Initially, I found it difficult to understand El's journey. Like many parents, I had preconceived notions about gender identity. Acknowledging my own biases and seeking education were crucial steps I had to take to move forward together with El. I embraced her gender identity, allowing her the freedom to choose and never attempting to shame her.

While I initially tried to discourage her from exploring her identity, I came to realise that my role was to offer unwavering love and support.

Embrace the Journey Together

Sometimes I questioned El's path simply because of my lack of understanding. The uniqueness of every child's journey should never be underestimated: external factors cannot reliably determine outcomes. No intervention would have made any difference to El's desired outcome; nor would being raised in a different culture; and neither would a two-parent family, despite what some say about single mothers and their boys' lack of male role models. Don't let anyone tell you otherwise.

You can make your child's journey easy or hard, depending on your actions. This journey can be challenging, filled with unique uncertainties for each family. The most important thing is to express your love and support unequivocally. Listen attentively and create a safe space for open communication, devoid of judgement. Learning, adapting, and growing as your child does is crucial on this journey, which has no map. Embrace your commitment to your child's well-being, and together you can navigate the path forward.

Even if you don't know how to best support your child, just listen. Don't worry if you make mistakes; we all do. I did.

I cannot stress enough the need to approach information with a critical mindset when studying transgender identities. While some sources might present biased or incomplete data, reputable organisations offer valuable resources and insights. There is little research that can give unequivocal answers to transgender parents, and there is much media sensationalism. In my research, a source, once found, often fell apart when confronted by a counter-source. This is one of the main reasons I have avoided quoting percentages and other metrics provided by research surveys, as I cannot prove they are reliable.

Here are some tips for responsible research:

- Seek information from established LGBTQ+ organisations.
- Look for websites with *.org* or *.gov* extensions. These are often non-profit or government sources.

- Pay attention to the date the information was published. Opt for recent studies and resources.

By being mindful of these factors, you can find reliable and up-to-date information to support your child and understand their journey better.

Establish Positive Communication and Boundaries

Open and honest communication with healthcare professionals is vital for your child to receive the best possible support. Share your child's history and experiences, but remember, qualified specialists should guide, not dictate, your child's journey. Their role is to listen attentively, understand your child's needs, and collaborate on a supportive care plan.

Every parent may establish boundaries within their family. However, these boundaries should never invalidate or discriminate against your child's identity. It's important to respect your child's authentic self and their right to express their identity, to establish boundaries and expectations in a loving and supportive way, and to have open and honest conversations with your child to understand their needs and perspectives.

By fostering an environment of love, respect, and open communication, you can navigate your own journey as a parent while supporting your child's well-being.

Find Your Joy

Find what brings you joy and makes you happy, whether it's running, dancing, painting, singing, spending time in nature, enjoying quiet time alone, or connecting with loved ones. Remember, you can't pour from an empty cup. When you take care of yourself, you'll be able to offer even greater support to your child. Put your oxygen mask on first, and then you can support others.

Respect Your Child's Identity

Being transgender is not a choice; it's an identity. When a child discovers their identity is at odds with societal expectations, this can be challenging, but it can also be a source of strength and pride. When loved ones accept and celebrate a child's authentic self, it empowers the transgender individual and fosters immense resilience. Refusing to acknowledge someone's authentic identity can cause immense pain.

Start from a Place of Belief

Approach your child's journey with belief. If your child says they are transgender, support them and create a safe space for them to explore their identity. If they express that someone is causing them pain, believe them and listen. If they seek help, trust them and work together to find resources.

Ask for Help

Asking for help is especially important if you're used to taking care of others. Remember that it is a sign of strength, not weakness. Emotional support, practical help, and information from trusted resources can lighten your load. People may not offer help unless you ask, so reach out. You might be surprised by how willing others are to step up and support you on this journey.

Acknowledge Your Emotions and Accept Your Feelings

Grant yourself permission to experience your emotions, regardless of what they may be. It's fine to weep, to be overwhelmed, or to find yourself bewildered. Holding back emotions can impede personal development and overall health. Instead, engage in activities that allow you to explore and express your feelings in a healthy way. This could involve journaling, talking to a trusted friend, seeking professional support, or engaging in creative activities. Remember, acknowledging your emotions is a vital part of processing and moving forward. We all feel better after a good cry!

Forgive Yourself and Move Forward

It's that simple: Forgive yourself. We all wish we could have done something different and better, and it's natural to regret not having done things differently. However, dwelling on regrets isn't productive. Embrace your journey, learn from your experiences, and remember that we all grow and evolve. Even mistakes can offer valuable lessons. Some of my most valued guidance originated in the mistakes I made.

51

LOOKING AHEAD

Thankfully, many of my fears for El didn't materialise. While most media outlets strive for respectful reporting on LGBTQ+ issues, inaccurate portrayals of young transgender people exist, and many of these fuelled my anxieties. Witnessing El's journey has opened my eyes to the vast spectrum of experiences faced by transgender youth.

While I once worried about El's future relationships, health, and overall well-being, I now have immense faith in her ability to thrive. We were fortunate to have the resources and support system that allowed us to navigate this journey together, creating a safe and loving environment for El. However, I recognise not everyone shares this privilege and that many face significant challenges.

While El's social class, race, and support network may have offered a buffer against some forms of marginalisation, navigating her identity hasn't been without challenges. She, like many transgender individuals, encountered prejudice, misunderstanding, and hurtful language. These experiences can be isolating and taxing, leaving scars that take time to heal.

The growing waiting times and limited access to transition-related healthcare in the UK are troubling. It is not a straightforward route, with longer and longer waiting lists and caution urged by specialists and our government. This stands in contrast to the values of democracy, human rights, and equality that our country upholds. Under the current conditions, it's difficult for trans people to access any sort of gender-related care through the NHS. Often, services are influenced by the outmoded idea that being trans is a mental health problem, not an identity. The NHS is falling drastically short in supporting trans and non-binary people.

Creating a More Inclusive World

Despite the current limitations of healthcare in the UK, El and I share the hope for a brighter future for transgender people. We can all work towards this goal by educating ourselves on transgender identities, challenging prejudice whenever we encounter it, and advocating for inclusive policies. Together, we can create a world where we celebrate and support transgender people for who they are.

Conspiracy theories, mockery, and cruelty won't achieve anything constructive. Instead, they're simply distressing and hurtful to transgender people, who experience high rates of anxiety and depression. Let's focus on building empathy and understanding.

The current political climate has brought transgender rights to the forefront of social media. The recent government guidance for schools failed to address concerns or provide clear direction.

Everyone should have the same opportunities to succeed in life, no matter who they are. Transgender people deserve the same rights and protections as everyone else. We're not asking for greater rights for transgender people, only equal ones.

Many of my family members still don't understand being trans, but we are all agreed upon one thing: El is a different person. El is thriving as her authentic self – happy, confident, and brimming with positive thoughts and plans for the future. A few years ago, if someone had offered me an opportunity to see only one of these qualities in El, I would have snatched at it gratefully. Now I see all of them in El, with pride and overwhelming joy.

Love and acceptance can create a world of difference. When we embrace others for who they truly are, everyone thrives.

52

CELEBRATING MY SIXTIETH

October 2023 marked a special moment for our family. El celebrated my sixtieth birthday party as her true self. The transformation wasn't just physical; it radiated from within. The joy El shared with her partner was gratifying. They support each other wholeheartedly. El's cousins couldn't quite find the words to describe the amazing transformation they witnessed. They had never seen El so confident, bursting with energy and enthusiasm. We filled the evening with laughter, conversation, and shared stories. El's happiness infected everyone, and we all departed with a profound sense of joy and comprehension. Everyone realised this had been the right decision for El all along.

As my family discussed and pondered El's journey over a cocktail or two, we came to the realisation that we often shared the same concerns about El's well-being during her transition. Fear of discomfort had kept me from voicing them, and a similar hesitation had caused my family to remain silent. Open and constructive communication could have created a more supportive environment for both El and me.

This lack of open communication within our family created unnecessary distance and worry. It's understandable that I was embarrassed to admit I wasn't coping. We all harboured the same anxieties and concerns, but silence prevented us from offering or receiving support. Their lack of response left me with a sense of being judged, and my lack of response made them think I was managing. It would have helped to talk.

Reflecting on the past, I continually realise that I could have gained advantages from seeking support during difficult moments. Some memories I've recalled are still hard to process and accept, but my sixtieth is one that I cherish.

El's journey wasn't without its hurdles. There were undoubtedly challenging moments, and the emotional toll was sometimes significant. El's sister also had to adjust to the changes, and navigating these complexities together took patience and understanding. However, this experience has transformed each of us in profound ways. Today, I'm filled with immense gratitude for the growth and deeper connections that this journey has brought us all.

El was always confident in her decision to transition. Once she had the resources to complete her chosen medical options, she never looked back. There were moments of fear and concern, but for El, not transitioning was a far scarier prospect.

Extensive research and experience from leading medical organisations support gender-affirming care, including social transition and, when appropriate, medical transition, as the most effective treatment for gender dysphoria. As always, we must keep in mind that every person's experience is unique. Patients and qualified healthcare professionals should develop treatment plans collaboratively, based on specific needs and goals, to ensure individualised care. Is it perfect? Maybe not for all. Is it better than the only alternatives, denial and conversion therapy? Unquestionably.

My experience has reaffirmed my belief that most people, despite initial discomfort, confusion, or disagreement, can understand the profound love a parent has for their child. While the UK certainly has areas where LGBTQ+ rights need further strengthening, I'm encouraged by positive changes and ongoing efforts.

The road to full equality for LGBTQ+ people in the UK may have some detours, and it's clear that progress requires continued advocacy. The fight for a ban on conversion therapy and for broader LGBTQ+ rights is more crucial than ever.

LGBTQ+ rights do not undermine freedom of speech or belief. Everyone is entitled to their opinions, but hate speech and harmful practices such as conversion therapy do not qualify as protected forms of expression. We can advocate for LGBTQ+ rights while also safeguarding children's well-being, women's rights, and respectful discourse.

I am proud of my daughter, El, and the courage she has shown every day. This journey has been a profound learning experience. It's fostered a deeper understanding of myself, revealing areas for growth and opportunities to learn. Through this experience, I've identified and challenged limiting beliefs I once held. Today, I cultivate self-compassion and love, mirroring the kindness I strive to extend to others. While I wasn't perfect, I take comfort in knowing I did my best with the knowledge and understanding I had.

Understanding and accepting my daughter's transgender identity was a gradual journey for me, which involved facing my own fears and biases. While I always loved and supported El, navigating this change wasn't always easy. It's natural to experience emotions like grief and loss when our children embark on journeys that differ from our expectations.

I cannot deny that there were difficult times. I loved having a son, and I quietly grieved for that loss. And sometimes I struggled to understand and accept my daughter's identity. But instead of clinging to outdated views, I committed to learning and growing alongside her. I hoped to be a source of unwavering support, even if I experienced uncertainty about the 'right' things to say or do.

I no longer worry about what other people think or try to fit or blend in. I found genuine friends, inner peace, and calm, and I have two daughters I am proud to say are mine.

My daughter tells me today, 'It isn't where you started the journey, Mum, but where you ended it.'

I am proud of where we stand today, and I remain committed to supporting El on her journey.

I share this personal story to offer a glimpse into the complexities of supporting a loved one through a significant personal journey. Individuals have varying perspectives, and this narrative does not seek to support or criticise any specific viewpoints. People can, and do, have different perspectives. Some may argue for transgender rights, and some for cisgender rights. But why does there have to be a choice? Shouldn't compassion, empathy, and understanding lead the way? Why are we not all advocating for a fairer, safer life for all?

Some of our relatives were filled with uncertainty and worry about the possibility of embarrassment or judgement when I started writing our story. I, too, was concerned about the potential danger of hate and violence being directed at us, but I still felt it was important to share this eventful and ultimately positive story. El was optimistic and eager to let her story be shared. We wanted to promote awareness and foster acceptance.

While writing our story and talking with El, I discovered there was quite a bit I was unaware of. I realised some of my casual comments were seen as critical and unsupportive, especially at the beginning. I now know acutely that El felt my negativity and defensive mentality.

Occasionally, when I didn't understand what was happening, I pretended that I did. I found myself in situations where I had to scramble to explain my emotions and reasoning to El. I often remained on the sidelines. I shut myself off from many things. In the beginning I let El down because I was trying to avoid the situation, hoping that it was only a phase. I was embarrassed and constricted by my beliefs. As a cisgender person, even though I support El now, I still don't completely grasp it all, and maybe I never will, but El and I are okay with that.

I am thankful to both my beautiful girls. Telling our story has been a privilege, an opportunity to share my immense pride in both of them.

The wonderful bond between El and Josie, filled with strength and unwavering support, is truly inspiring. Together, they both were my rock when I needed them. Their unwavering love and support mean the world to me.

El and Josie, there are no words to describe how wonderful you both are. The genuine kindness, support, and loyalty you showed during some of the tumultuous periods fill me with immense pride. Our journey has brought growth to everyone. I'm incredibly proud of the strong, compassionate women you are. I can't wait to see what amazing things you each accomplish in the future.

EPILOGUE

El Embraces Her Authentic Self

El's confidence has soared since embracing her true identity. She's now running a dog hotel, a perfect fit for her compassion and love for animals. El is also happy to share her experiences and offer support to others on their journeys. Her family remains her biggest cheerleader, offering unwavering love and admiration.

Experiencing a sense of comfort and confidence with her identity, El recently joined a gym. She's excited about building her physical strength and stamina.

El's partner has been a constant source of strength throughout her transition, a rock of unwavering love and acceptance. Together, they're planning exciting adventures. El excitedly discusses wearing a swimsuit on holiday, a simple act that once caused anxiety but now symbolises new confidence. Their family is growing now that they've welcomed a six-year-old rescue dog from the local shelter. Their cosy home, once filled with the quiet hum of El's self-doubt, now echoes with the sounds of playful paws and joyous barks. El's transformation profoundly inspires those around her, as her self-acceptance permeates every aspect of her life.

El's Voice

All I wanted was to be at peace with who I am. I wished for the person I saw in the mirror to reflect who I truly was.

I faced many difficulties during my journey. I felt a strong desire to move forward, but deep inside, fear often gripped me, and I was unsure whether this decision would lead me in the right direction. I had faith in it, but I was fearful it wasn't true. I continuously struggled to make sense of things. I thought having a more female anatomy would make me feel better, but I wondered whether it would completely ease my body dysphoria. I was also scared of the pain and the discomfort and potential complications associated with the surgical procedures. Looking at myself in the mirror now, I can't help but feel thrilled. When people interact with me, they see my authentic self. I've embraced authenticity and stopped pretending.

I enjoy selecting clothes from my sister's fashion collection, and occasionally Josie sends me a freebie! I also feel fortunate to have a partner who sees me as sexy and appealing. People no longer refer to me as handsome.

One of my counsellor's first questions, a simple yet profound one, was, 'Imagine a button that takes you where you long to be – would you push it?' I can still feel the gravity of that moment. My response was immediate and unmistakable: Yes.

If I were asked that question now, considering everything, my immediate response would be a firm no. The physical agony, the moments of utter despair, and the struggles I've faced – I regret none of it, for each taught me something invaluable. The collective weight of these experiences, each with its distinct feel and impact, has moulded me into the person I am today. Every step of the journey, from the challenges overcome to the lessons learned, was just as crucial as the final result.

It was a tough journey, but the rewards were worthwhile. I cannot express enough how grateful I am for the continuous encouragement and assistance I receive from my family and friends, particularly my mother. I know that you faced challenges and doubts initially, but to me, you were everything. Everything I have, I owe to you.

Me

Today, I revel in a happiness that surpasses anything I've known before. Releasing control and embracing the flow has brought about a profound change.

From Seeking Answers to Finding Myself

When I started therapy, my intention was to address what I perceived as imperfections in my life. I believed a relationship was the answer and that counselling would unveil the reasons my past relationships had failed. My career success and financial independence seemed like markers of achievement, sufficient validation. However, therapy brought me to a far more profound realisation: I didn't need a relationship to be complete.

Instead, I cultivated a fulfilling relationship with myself. Therapy led me to a much deeper truth: I was already whole, regardless of external validation. I am enough, I now know with unwavering conviction. Singleness seems like the appropriate path for now, and I have confidence that love will find me when the time is right, with me prepared to embrace it with emotional maturity.

Embracing Change and Purpose

My journey has been one of self-discovery and shedding unnecessary things. Trading a career in learning support for teaching brought a deeper sense of purpose and fulfilment. Releasing my house, a representation of accomplishment with which I had a deep personal connection, was a pivotal moment. Downsizing felt liberating, a lesson in detachment from material possessions. Moving into a rented space solidified the realisation that true value lies beyond ownership. Now, I'm taking the next step by selling my business and pursuing a career as a personal development coach. This shift reflects my desire to prioritise joy and purpose over financial gain.

Embracing Joy in the Present

Joy infuses everything I do, from invigorating workouts and nature walks to the laughter I share with Josie while we renovate our houses and the cheers I exchange with El during Formula 1 races. Every day brings a sense of fulfilment. Restoring furniture and transforming my cottage and garden provide a deep sense of accomplishment, while quiet moments spent meditating amid the fragrant blooms offer pure bliss.

Surrounded by the love and support of incredible friends and family, I cherish the peace that comes with embracing the present moment. What a journey it's been! I am thankful for it.

The experience of raising a transgender child has influenced how I view and approach coaching. As a personal development coach, I now specialise in supporting parents of transgender individuals, drawing on my own experiences to guide them with empathy and understanding. My goal is to empower others on similar journeys.

Be strong, compassionate, and open to change. Life may just surprise you!

GLOSSARY

Acquired gender is a phrase sometimes used to refer to the gender in which a transgender person lives and presents to the world. This is not the gender to which they were assigned at birth, but it is the gender they should be treated as possessing.

Agender denotes or relates to a person who does not identify as having a gender.

Asexual describes a person who experiences no sexual feelings or desires.

Biological sex refers to a person's gender assigned at birth.

Blockers, or puberty blockers, are medicines that prevent puberty from happening.

Breast augmentation is also known as augmentation mammoplasty. This is surgery to increase breast size.

Cross-dresser refers to someone who wears clothing usually characteristic of the 'opposite' gender. Other terms include *transvestite* (now dated) and *dual role*. Cross-dressers usually are not transgender and do not seek medical intervention.

Cisgender denotes or relates to a person whose gender identity corresponds with the sex assigned to them at birth.

Gender binary refers to the concept of male and female as either/or identities; it does not allow for or recognise other experiences of gender.

Gender diverse describes a person whose gender identity or gender expression does not conform to socially defined male or female gender norms.

Gender dysphoria is the term for a deep sense of unease and distress that may occur when your assigned gender at birth does not match your gender identity.

Gender expression is how a person publicly expresses or presents their gender.

Gender identity describes how a person feels about their gender. For many people, their gender identity corresponds to the sex they were registered at birth. For others, it does not.

Genderqueer refers to someone who doesn't follow binary gender norms.

Gender affirmation refers to processes used by trans people to live as their chosen gender.

Gender reassignment is the term used by the Equality Act to refer to the process used to reassign one's sex to accord with identity rather than the sex assigned to a person at birth.

Gender recognition certificate is a certificate issued under the Gender Recognition Act that enables trans people to be legally recognised in their acquired gender.

FFS is an abbreviation for feminine facial surgery.

LGBTQ+ is an abbreviation that encompasses numerous identities: lesbian, gay, bisexual, transgender, and queer (or questioning), plus many other terms (such as non-binary and pansexual). Other variations, such as LGBTQIA or LGBTQIA+, are also used.

Medical transitioning refers to physically changing one's body, either temporarily or permanently, through medical procedures so it will align with one's gender identity.

Non-binary is used to describe people who feel their gender cannot be defined by the gender binary.

Sexual orientation refers to the emotional, romantic, or sexual attraction that a person feels toward another person.

Social transitioning involves changing a person's name and/or pronouns, appearance or expression (such as clothing or hairstyles), behaviours, and so on.

Tomboy is a term used for girls or young women with masculine traits; this is distinct from gender identity.

Trans is a short form of *transgender*. A transgender person is someone whose gender identity differs from that associated with the sex they were assigned at birth.

Transsexual is a now outdated term most closely associated with the legally protected characteristic of having undergone gender reassignment. A transsexual person may be a person assigned female at birth who has transitioned or is transitioning to identify as a man, or a person assigned male at birth who has transitioned or is transitioning to live as a woman. The law does not require a person to undergo a medical procedure to be recognised as a transsexual person. This term is now considered offensive by some.

Transgender men are female-to-male transgender people. In other words, a transgender man was assigned female at birth but has a male gender identity.

Transgender women are male-to-female transgender people. In other words, a transgender woman was assigned male at birth but has a female gender identity.

Transition is the process by which a transgender person permanently adopts the outward or physical characteristics that match their gender identity, as opposed to those associated with the sex registered for them at birth.

Note that terms such as *tranny, shemale, pre-op, post-op, gender-bender,* and *hermaphrodite* are considered dated or offensive. In the case of words such as *tranny, shemale, hermaphrodite,* and *gender-bender,* these are considered offensive because they've historically been used in dehumanising or inaccurate ways. In the case of terms such as *pre-op* and *post-op,* this terminology is seen as reducing people to their surgical status rather than acknowledging their identity.

USEFUL RESOURCES RELATED TO TRANSGENDER ISSUES

- The World Professional Association for Transgender Health, a professional organisation devoted to the treatment of transgender people, publishes *The Standards of Care for Gender Identity Disorders*, which offers recommendations for the provision of gender affirmation procedures and services. It can be accessed here: https://www.wpath.org/publications/soc.

- For advice to help you understand what gender identity is and how to support a child, visit the National Society for the Prevention of Cruelty to Children at https://www.nspcc.org.uk/keeping-children-safe/sex-relationships/gender-identity/.

- The Mix provides essential support for those under twenty-five. Understand the different issues young transgender people face and where to get needed support: https://www.themix.org.uk/sex-and-relationships/gender-and-sexuality/young-and-trans-5178.html.

- LGBT Youth Scotland provides online forums discussing everything LGBTQ+ related, helping LGBTQ+ young people to flourish and thrive: https://lgbtyouth.org.uk/.

- The Beaumont Society offers a twenty-four seven information line with regional organizers who can point you toward the best resources for you. Their mission is to create a supportive and inclusive environment for all transgender individuals: https://beaumontsociety.org/.

- For details of LGBTQ+ milestones in law, consult this University and College Union resource: https://www.ucu.org.uk/media/11041/LGBTlegislation/pdf/LGBT_legal_milestones_FINAL.pdf.

- The Equality and Human Rights Commission monitors human rights, protecting equality across nine grounds: age, disability, sex, race, religion, and belief. Information regarding these can be found here: http://www.equalityhumanrights.com.

- Read HM Government's transgender action plan, a document setting out specific actions across government to advance transgender equality, here: https://assets.publishing.service.gov.uk/media/5a79d132ed915d6b1deb38f7/transgender-action-plan.pdf.

- Trans Europe and Central Asia provides details of campaigns and rights being fought for in Europe: https://tgeu.org.

- The Gender Identity Research & Education Society is a UK-wide organisation whose purpose is to improve the lives of trans and gender-diverse people of all ages, including those who are non-binary and non-gender: http://www.gires.org.uk.

- Read the House of Commons Women and Equalities Committee Transgender Equality report (2015–2016) here: https://publications.parliament.uk/pa/cm201516/cmselect/cmwomeq/390/390.pdf.

- Wikipedia provides useful information on gender-affirming surgery (https://en.wikipedia.org/wiki/Gender-affirming_surgery) and facial feminization surgery (https://en.wikipedia.org/wiki/Facial_feminization_surgery).

Facialteam Marbella

Ventura del Mar 11
29660 Nueva Andalucía
Marbella, Spain
Tel: +34 952 898 842
help@facialteam.eu

PERSONAL GROWTH RESOURCES

Podcasts

- The Positive Head Podcast (https://www.positivehead.com) helps to maintain a positive headspace.

- Letting Go & The Greatest Secret (https://lettinggo.libsyn.com) is a podcast with Hale Dwoskin for those suffering with uncertainty, anxiety, or pain.

- The Inner Child Podcast (https://bygloriazhang.com) is a self-help series by Gloria Zhang, an inner child healer, therapist, relationship coach, TEDx speaker, and author. I used this podcast when undertaking my inner child work. It helped with visualising techniques and my understanding of how child trauma can affect adult life.

- Awareness Explorers (https://www.awarenessexplorers.com) helps listeners embrace the joy and peace of awareness in daily life.

- Oprah's Super Soul (https://podcasts.apple.com/us/podcast/oprahs-super-soul/id1264843400) collects Oprah's inspiring interviews with thought leaders, bestselling authors, spiritual figures, and experts on health and well-being.

- A Changed Mind Podcast (https://www.youtube.com/ playlist?list=PL_28j4T1NX3_qUKAcs4Jsg_edcRvwU7QX) by David Bayer discusses topics from neuroscience, personal growth, health, and relationships, to global issues such as the environment, censorship, and democracy.

- Although Dr Joe Dispenza (https://drjoedispenza.com), who researches epigenetics, quantum physics, and neuroscience, doesn't have a formal podcast, his free information and meditations on YouTube help calm the mind and encourage emotional growth and a positive mindset.

- Lewis Howes's The School of Greatness Podcast (https:// lewishowes.com/sogpodcast/) features great interviews with world-renowned leaders in business, entertainment, sports, science, health, and literature, inspiring listeners to unlock inner greatness and live their best lives.

Books

Some of these books were recommended by my counsellor, and others I found myself. All helped me to understand emotions, limited beliefs, and the complexities and limitations of our minds.

- *The Language of Emotions,* by Karlak McLaren, is a great book to help you understand the full range of emotions we possess and learn to live with all of them.

- *Daring Greatly,* by Brené Brown, was the foundational text of my healing journey; I remember the weight of the book in my hands as I began to read. It changed my perspective, profoundly altering my understanding of myself and the world. I then immersed myself in reading *Rising Strong* and *Braving the Wilderness.* Each provided further help with personal growth and the understanding of my limiting beliefs, offering insights that were both challenging and rewarding.

- *Brave Thinking,* by Mary Morrissey, promises to 'upgrade your mind to upgrade your life.' I found it inspiring and a powerful aid in my journey.

Spirituality Resources

The books listed below cover a diverse array of spiritual subjects. I enjoyed them, even though they differed from my usual reading preferences. All helped me in moving from a negative to a positive mindset.

- In *The Little Book of Buddhism,* the Dalai Lama offers his insights on Buddhism. I have always been interested in Buddhism and found these insightful.

- In *The Golden Key*, Brandon Beachum explores the concept of unlocking infinite abundance. I discovered this through the Positive Head Podcast. Well worth the read.

- In *The Enlightenment Project*, Jonathan Robinson provides insights on awakening gleaned from interviews with teachers such as the Dalai Lama, Byron Katie, Deepak Chopra, Mother Teresa, and Ram Dass.

- In *Autobiography of a Yogi*, Yogananda Paramahansa offers profound and beautifully written insights into spirituality and yoga.

- In *The Freedom of Being*, Jan Frazier offers practical tips for remaining in the present.

- In *When Fear Falls Away*, Jan Frazier tells the story of her own personal awakening.

- In *Opening the Door*, Jan Frazier explores the nature of spiritual awakening and the possibilities of life.

- In *Happiness Is Free*, Lester Levenson and Hale Dwoskin provide insights and practical tools to help us let go of painful feelings, unwanted thoughts, and negative stories, thus opening up to happiness and potential.

- In *The Power of Intention*, Dr Wayne Dyer taught me, 'Change the way you look at things and the things you look at will change.' This book explores intention, not as something you do but as an energy you're part of.

- In *Breaking the Habit of Being Yourself*, Dr Joe Dispenza provides step-by-step tools for remaking your mind and your life.